Rhythms Of An Impenitent Life

Ian Gant

AuthorHouse™
1663 Liberty Drive, Suite 200
Bloomington, IN 47403
www.authorhouse.com
Phone: 1-800-839-8640

©*2008 Ian Gant. All rights reserved.*

No part of this book may be reproduced, stored in a retrieval system, or transmitted by any means without the written permission of the author.

First published by AuthorHouse   8/11/2008

ISBN: 978-1-4343-7682-4 (sc)
ISBN: 978-1-4343-7683-1 (hc)

Printed in the United States of America
Bloomington, Indiana

This book is printed on acid-free paper.

To My Dear Wife
Jacqueline
For Her Continuing Care and Affection
And
To My Children and Grandchildren
That Someday They Might Understand

Contents

Foreword vii
With Affection 1
A Yorkshire Living 37
No Argument With The Gods 109
The Politics of Humour 179

Foreword

Though for more than twenty years the resident of a small and very rural North Yorkshire village I was born and had all my education in the greater city of the West Riding. A product of my time I can look back on many eventful years as both observer and participant in the social and political activities of both these counties.

The second son of a seagoing engineering officer and a minor union official I was raised in an Anglo / Italian household dominated by a powerful mother and my resourceful but remarkably volatile grandmother.

During a varied adult life I have felt the strictures of uniformed service sold my soul to the marketeers in the pursuit of money and was employed for a period by the UK's most famous private psychiatric hospital.

Having concluded that it is never enough to be satisfied by the mundane or the obvious curiosity has filled my life and though variously this has brought me to adventure and discomfort it has remarkably never come near to killing this peculiar cat.

Fortunate but never lucky I have known the love or at least the loving of many women but as often as I fell into that rapture I found myself in stormy seas. Though somewhat unconventional my second marriage has brought me to a safe haven and being at last chaste and chastened my anchorage is now in calm and sheltered waters.

A creature of spirit my internal argument has always been between the inner dogmatist and the incorrigible romantic who surfaces when the toil of day is done.

I cannot and do not try to offer solutions; my verse is simply a comment on my experience; if I offend I do not regret it and if

I provoke then so much to the good.

IG

With Affection

A Bluebird of Happiness

We had a car a basic thing,
Its metal wrapped us like a glove,
While from its seats we watched the world,
The world saw strangers fall in love.

One hundred thousand miles and more,
Of coast and city, vale and hill,
From burst of spring to summer heat,
Through autumn gold and winter chill.

We were not conscious of the craft,
That built this thing to mans design,
But revelled in the magnitude,
Of what became just hers and mine.

The simple days of work and play,
The dangers that our lives surround,
A pleasure that the world displays,
A box of steel on holy ground.

And when at last it had to go,
We hid a note for latter days,
That read upon the wrecking time,
Would speak of love and lovers ways.

This poets view, this thing of words,
Transports from pristine back to rust,
But words remain when cars are scrap,
When all is done and we are dust.

With thanks to the men and women of Nissan at Washington

A Reflection on Rising From Sleep

When we confuse the love in life,
With longing or with lust,
We offer passions paltry sum,
Instead of truth and trust.

We reap where we refused to sow,
To bitter harvests stored,
With futures mortgaged to a cause,
The love of gold as lord.

A gordian knot a misers chain,
Each binding us apart,
Till life with wisdom's last refrain,
Sends arrows to the heart.

The footsteps from the gates of hell,
A hands breadth from the grave,
With aching past to pull us down,
And lives ahead to save.

So give us all just time enough,
With time enough to spare,
And teach us all to love enough,
With love enough to care.

And These Three

To be at peace, to be at home,
Where faith and hope and love abide,
Then we may all of heaven know,
In sanctity beyond divide.

A creatures grace a tender word,
A refuge in a stormy sea,
When I am all that you can know,
And you are all in all to me.

When I was lost you held me safe,
With arms the rage could not defy,
And I was comfort in your sway,
In passion I could not deny.

The clouds that come to hinder sight,
Will rain a sadness in my heart,
For days will come when we are old,
And days will come when we must part.

So I must ask for time enough,
To rest forever in your sigh,
For time will never be enough,
Till time enough to say goodbye.

Beginnings

If you have peace within your heart,
Speak gentle soft and low,
And I will follow close my love,
Wherever you may go.

If you can find a quiet place,
Where none may know your name,
Then I would seek to be with you,
Deserting pride and fame.

If you would take me all in all,
And conquer all desire,
Then I could want for nothing more,
Than warmth within your fire.

If you could see me with my eyes,
My shadow on your mind,
Then I would throw the world away,
And be in passion blind.

If you will lead me day by day,
And year by year by year,
Then I will know eternity,
And conquer every fear.

Colours of Life

When I was young, so very young,
And childish dreams filled every night,
Then innocence was just a word,
And all of love was blossom white.

Then in my teens at odds confused,
When urgent life made spirits mean,
A user used and used again,
When love was bold and emerald green.

Cold comfort years of joy and pain,
Some times a leader sometimes led,
Wild star of life that flares and flames,
Where all of love is poppy red.

Then aging, feeling month and year,
Both weak and willing false and true,
With passions fading day by day,
With love so pale and cornflower blue.

But in the end the world has turned,
And comforts me as I grow old,
And brings me to a kinder earth,
Where love is bright and burnished gold.

Dancing

I never have taken her dancing,
Though the music is sensual sweet,
I never have taken her dancing,
Though we move to a mystical beat.

It's like holding hands in the moonlight,
On a beach where the sand shimmers gold,
When you know there is nothing tomorrow,
And you're sure you will never grow old.

There's a softer caress than the kissing,
There's a passion that holds you within,
There is life to surround and enfold you,
There is subtlety yearning to win.

When the melody masks all the meaning,
And we mingle like stars in the night,
We will touch like the song of creation,
And be born to a world of delight.

Like Pan in the fields of the ageless,
Where his children were many and few,
I am loved with great glory abandon,
And am father to all that is true.

For the satyrs and nymphs once emboldened,
Are like waves that crash bright on the shore,
And the song that I hear they are singing,
Is bidding me dance evermore.

There will be no more time for the dancing,
When the fire in our hearts turns to chill,
There will be no more time for the dancing,
When the music of time fails to thrill.

When the wind blows the sand on the seashore,
Into dunes that young lovers can't climb,
And the shadows encompass the moonlight,
And the tawdry supplants the sublime.

So I claw at the stars in the heaven,
As they dance in eternities round,
And the music that echoes around me,
Is the revel of hominid sound.

For the softer caress still supports me,
As we move to the mystical beat,
And I know in some way we are dancing,
With the whole of the world at our feet.

I never have taken her dancing,
Though we turn and we whirl and we spin,
And the music goes on never ending,
While we wait for the ball to begin.

Fortress

I turn all the pages and read every line,
Of a life filled with fortune but never with luck,
And I contemplate chapters that chronicle me.
When time was the issue and I was the book.

I have hung from the gallows and stared at the crowd,
With pleasure a shadow and duty a noose,
In a place that knew nothing of solace or sin,
With life the abuser and I the abuse.

A creature of passions but emptied to pain,
With truth an illusion mans vanity sure,
While vision was jaundiced and charity gone,
And poverties pressure the grace of the poor.

Yet there waited a splendour, a rapture, a hope,
In the midst of the battle a refuge a keep,
Where demons are captured and shackled and chained,
And I was the dreamer enabled to sleep.

I have come to the mountain where all men are free,
To the fountain eternal that trumpets of peace,
With my hand in her hand who carried me home,
And the whisper of wonders that gave me release.

There is grace in her laughter and hope in her eyes,
And she is my vision, my brightest and best,
For captured, enraptured, surrounded and safe,
I stand here enchanted, ennobled and blessed.

I fear not the shadows of gallows or block,
For my haven is real and is where I belong,
A sanctuary builded with hope at its heart,
With love as its battlements making me strong.

From Bitter Fields

I ploughed on the farm of destruction,
I reaped while the flags were furled,
I cried with the words unspoken,
And I tore at the staves of the world.

My grief was in lost tears of sorrow,
For the sentinel proud by my grave,
And I gave what I had of nothing,
With nothing and no one to save.

But a stranger at hand in the darkness,
Had staved off the blows with a kiss,
And rounded me safe in her shadow,
And found me the meaning of bliss.

No heaven contains such emotion,
No hell could consume with such fire,
As I give and I live and I languish,
In this treasure of pain and desire.

And yet I would change not a moment,
I will beg for the years not to end,
For sustained as I am and surrounded,
In my passion my love and my friend.

Grace And Thistledown

So it is to be in love,
Not in first flush all passion bright,
But gentle love that stirs the soul,
And comforts in the blackest night.

Love as light as thistledown,
Yet stronger than a mighty tree,
That holds as fast as the clinging vine,
But only serves to set you free.

Sweet selfless love so foolish wise,
That even saints would call a grace,
Where earthly treasures I despise,
And find redemption in their place.

Wild willing love that bears no chain,
Creating as the lightning flies,
That understands the joys of man,
Forgiving truth, deceiving lies.

Yet knowing love and being love,
All wrapped within a boundless sway,
My heaven is within her arms,
Till god shall steal my breath away.

Hands

When angels fly on broken wings,
The heavens roar with thunder,
And earth is washed in bloodless rain,
As clouds are broke asunder.

For friendships are like angels wings,
Ethereal as summer breeze,
We build them up as fortresses,
And cut them down like shattered trees.

Companionship is burdens proof,
That breaking bread is sweet caress,
A sacrament or mouldering crumb,
Salvations gate, or something less.

My childhood friends feed timeless joy,
This not forgotten treasured past,
Of woodland walks and pleasured hills,
Of hidden caves and fish lines cast.

The pure affections of the child,
Bring succour to the falling soul,
The stain that taints the virgins ground,
Will heal the part and wound the whole.

And I am wounded with the rest,
By avarice and pride and lust,
The sweetest lips are all in vain,
When they have crumbled into dust.

But yet we still stretch out the hand,
With hard clenched fist or open palm,
A sword cuts free the olive branch,
We speed to bless and rush to harm.

But then again the sun filled days,
Of innocence and quiet dreams,
When I could love without regret,
As so it was, as so it seems.

We can't go back and nor we should,
Our hair turns grey our eyes grow dull,
And wanton love all once sublime,
Is turned to something fine and full.

We walk with true companionship,
Who break the bread and drink the wine,
The hand that weakens still has truth,
When that frail hand is placed in mine.

Holding On

We hold each other and are strong,
When night is deep and all is calm,
When sleep is just a dream away,
And comes no fright and no alarm.

In tenderness as light as down,
Complete in comfort soft and warm,
Where there is everything and love,
And comes no worry and no storm.

To be as one quite bound but free,
Is heaven better or more sure,
Where then to seek the inner calm,
And comes the joy that will endure.

To touch, to feel, to understand,
Some deity in all mankind,
When consternation fades away,
And comes a blessing to the mind.

We hold each other and are strong,
No raging demon stands between,
Where we have touched a different plane,
And come to peace that few have seen.

Hope

I'm looking for the killing fields,
The stranger said to me,
The ridge of stone is cold and bare,
And barren stands the tree,
I wander on a dismal plain,
Mans monuments are rust,
And all his creativity,
Is vanity and dust.

I took him gently by the hand,
And led him to a hill,
To see the children playing there,
Quite heedless of the chill,
I took him to a quiet place,
Where humble people pray,
And when I looked into his eyes,
He turned and looked away.

Who are you then he said to me,
For I am death and pain,
I ever walk this earth alone,
And all its powers retain,
I turned and to the stranger said,
With me mankind can cope,
For I am your own brother,
And my children call me hope.

Imo Pectore

When half asleep and waiting dawn,
I sense her presence close and calm,
And that brings sweet awakening,
To gently soften all alarm.

For love came slow but diamond hard,
And softer than a pure pearl blush,
Too precious for the light of day,
Too sacred for the cloisters hush.

This woman's want this thing of clay,
Intoxication, fire and flame,
When love is wanton wild and free,
Desire puts word and wit to shame.

Reclined, enraptured, slow to stir,
I contemplate her sleeping grace,
And capture in my inner mind,
What is for me my time and space.

A woman certain, gentle, brave,
Both frail and faulted, bold and bright,
Within whose arms I melt away,
And all my weakened will requite.

True love is not a passing thing,
It wraps you, folds you, binds you tight,
It burns like acid, chills like rain,
But keeps you in the darkest night.

So what of this, and what of that,
Emotions puppet, no not I,
I hold the real and touch the truth,
To see the world from where I lie.

I rise from bed; she stirs, then still,
And wistful I prepare the day,
Where we not parted but apart,
Must love from many miles away.

It

It comes to wound; it rides the storm,
It turns you round; it points the way,
It folds your mind; it makes you still,
It binds the hours; it holds the day.

It teaches nothing you would learn,
It ends beginnings with a sigh,
It makes the truth a poet's tale,
It sanctifies the oldest lie.

It winds confusion round your soul,
It lifts you up on ageless wings,
It speaks in riddles lost for words
It writes the song the angel sings.

It ties you down; it sets you free,
It drowns the night with bitter tears,
It calms the heart; it fires the blood,
It brings you low; it ends your fears.

It tells of joy; it brings you pain,
It scorns all wisdom from above,
It locks the door; it finds the key,
It breaks the chain; for it is love.

Lovers in Another May

Come take my hand and we will go,
To places we have never seen,
To where the crystal rivers flow,
In valleys soft and verdant green.

Come take my hand and walk with me,
Into a world that's yours and mine,
A promise of things yet to be,
For Harlequin and Columbine.

Come take my hand and hold me near,
And lead me to the ageless sea,
For you alone can still my fear,
And you alone can set me free.

Come take my hand and you will know,
In still of night or rush of day,
When I have lost the words to show,
How well I loved you in the May.

Read at my wedding and never forgot.

Marriage Rite

They say there's no love without passion,
And you cannot melt steel without flame,
Where there is no reward without struggle,
And the tiger was not made to tame.

When you cut me I bleed and I suffer,
When you kiss me I melt like the snow,
When you hold me I grasp life eternal,
When rejected I've nowhere to go.

The touch of your lips is a torture,
That caresses both body and mind,
And the laughter that flies from your anger,
Is the light in the eyes of the blind.

I came to this world cold and naked,
Like a worm from the edge of a grave,
A freeman who cries in the darkness,
Being bound by the chains of a slave.

Bright gold on a sinister finger,
A book and a nuptial prayer,
In the ritual of wanton awakening,
Is the field of the wheat and the tare.

And thus we are part in each other,
In the blood at the heart of the earth,
By this curse and this blessing corrupted,
We will bring all our essence to birth.

I am locked in the jaws of the tiger,
I am hot melted steel from the flame,
Being lost in the wild blessed struggle,
With the woman who carries my name.

No Coin for The Ferryman

It should have been a flaming June,
But the deluge was never still,
The days were waiting the summer sun,
The hours a way to kill.

We carried no coin for the ferryman,
As we went to visit her there,
She was lost and we were losing,
In a world that didn't care.

She asked us "am I dying",
We told her a needless lie,
She bade us love each other,
She bade us both goodbye.

And death did not come easy,
It was fight while minutes last,
For what do you leave but memories,
When the rush of life is past.

We stood with the rain in our faces,
It was masking the tears as we cried,
For we both felt shut and empty,
The day that mother died.

For my late mother Diamira Gant

Of Life

I drink her in like the sweet red wine,
I smell her scent on the summer breeze,
I hold her close as the clinging vine,
I hear her voice in the rustling trees,

For she is summer young and bold,
And she is summer wild and free,
And nothing in her could be old,
For she is light and love to me.

I call to her where the blossoms flame,
I seek her out where the tall reeds blow,
And in the meadow speak her name,
And touch the earth where her flowers grow.

I drink her in like the sweet red wine,
For she is summer wild and free,
For years to come she will be mine,
For she is ever part of me.

Pyramid

I saw that the sphinx was smiling,
Though I reasoned no reason why,
As we stood by the ancient wonders,
Under the cloudless sky.

We had crossed the sea by moonlight,
Soft as a maiden's hair,
Each wave was our bed of blossom,
Each tide was our time to care.

Yet standing in the desert,
Gazed on by sightless eyes
Four thousand years of passion,
Proclaiming our age of lies.

You love and then you are forgotten,
And none may remember your name,
For what is the true face of passion,
When facing the sword and the flame.

It was then that I first saw the message,
In the way that the old one had smiled,
That love in the world will be endless,
While we are by that loving beguiled.

Resolution

I noticed today that the swallows had gone,
Something of winter had burdened the sky,
A thorn apple grows in the closed wasted land,
But unlike the swallows it's fruitless to fly.

This realisation is gentle and kind,
Like the comfort of clothing full fitted and worn,
Like the sweetness of wine that's full bodied and ripe,
Like the scent of a hay barn with mouldering corn.

For reality tells me that all must be so,
And a south flying swallow may never return,
For all things of passage must pass to an end,
And for fire to have ashes the forest must burn.

For each and for every there must be a close,
And for each and for every a last bloom of spring,
From the last shock of snow at the edge of the wood,
To the final dawn chorus the blackbird will sing.

But spare me the knowledge for nothing should tell,
Of the last time I lie with the woman I love,
Of the last time her arms wrap me close as a prayer,
Of the last time a hawk will be chased by the dove,

Of the last time I see that the swallows have gone,
Of the last time I've tasted the full bodied wine,
Of the last time I face down the troubles within,
And cast out my demons in gadarine swine.

It is said that we may not know timing or place,
Lest we wait for the volley the rope or the block,
The mightiest mystery waits in the dark,
The light of the heavens, the shimmering shock.

Full precious the minute, full precious the hour,
Full precious the year and the month and the day,
Full precious the sunlight, the warm winds that blow,
Full precious the evening that steals them away.

I know it is coming I know it will come,
Like a curse and a thief it will plunder my dreams,
Like a witch with enchantments it circles me round,
And pulls at my clothing to sunder the seams.

I have life without fortune, but fortunate still,
I have loved in the living both fulsome and fair,
Caressed in the moonlight by calm watchful seas,
And kissed the most gentle to empty my care.

So why should I envy the swallows that fly,
For contentment is comfort for body and soul,
The thorn apple grows on the closed wasted land,
But I am at peace and my spirit is whole.

So look through the seasons and look to the south,
For the swallows return when the summer is near,
From a life in abundance I offer this creed,
As the sacrament hope and the sacrifice fear.

River

The vessel was dry and empty,
As the spirit was fettered and cold,
And you can't pour love from an empty soul,
When the sheep scatter far from the fold.

I would be on the hillside of blessings,
As a mendicant lost in the crowd,
A dreamer adrift on a broad sea of truth,
A schemer cast down by the proud.

What peace I may give is my armour,
A breastplate and sword for the fight,
When the spirit is tortured by anger,
And so little is left of the light.

The love that I send is my rampart,
A wall that no evil can breach,
And I walk in the steps of the angels,
To the river I never may reach.

To the stream that will carry me upward,
To the ocean of hope that I crave,
But I fear that I may never find it,
At least, not this side of the grave.

Sonata

She is the music of my life,
With songs eternal from her eyes,
Where wisdom walks within her streets,
And I am wanton with the wise.

For held but drowning in her arms,
Soft cadence in each breath I take,
When constancy is holy pride,
In love so deep a soul must ache.

To work with words and set their weave,
With thread as strong as iron will,
I push the bounds and force the line,
When all is grist to passions mill.

Sweet comfort then to those who know,
Love though requited still burns bright,
What symphonies of joy and pain,
Will pleasure in the darkest night.

And in the midst when wrapped in sound,
One note of rapture like a flame,
When justice is the shout of life,
And we are scales without a name.

We sing in chorus and are gone,
To pride and passion love and pain,
Our song remains the melody,
That none will ever hear again.

Spirit

I walked with the beast inside me,
Deep in my breath and bone,
Living his life from within me,
Always and ever alone.

The anger sustaining endurance,
Author of all my care,
Hunter when I was hunted,
Architect of my despair.

Feeding on my compassion,
The sound in him drove me on,
Eating away at my justice,
Waiting when hope had gone.

Ghost that he was and spirit,
Faded from me and past,
Hope his annihilation,
Joy my escape at last.

Here love has served to release me,
Freed from the haunt of night,
I walk with a truer companion,
Into the new realm of light.

Together

They say there is no perfection,
And faulted things must fail,
That wit and wonder fade away,
That rainbow colours pale.

And yet in my true beacon,
The flickering of the flame,
Is warmth and summer season,
And honour to my name.

My gift may not be worthy,
That cannot be denied,
To offer truth and constancy,
Where oft the world has lied.

This rhyme will seal our contract,
This verse in the written word,
A poor thing though to contemplate,
When better songs are heard.

Not perfect then but faulted,
In pride to set above,
And touch in this humanity,
The essence of my love.

Twilight Hours

And then she said "I love the twilight hours,"
When early spring is burdened in the air,
When blossom trees are stunned by hidden flowers,
And childhood bliss can banish every care.

I saw her mind as clearly as my own,
This woman both enigma and my wife,
Where in her joy and passion both atone,
Her clarity and wisdom fill my life.

As ageless and intangible as cloud,
She shadows but not casts me in the shade,
I hold and yet am held corrupt but proud,
And everything I make by her is made.

We drove the fading light as evening fell,
The conversation faltered with my thought,
I said "remind me soon and I will tell",
What heart has felt and intellect has taught.

I love her and there's little else to write,
I tell her and the words seem poor and vain,
I pondered as the twilight slipped to night,
The words she said resounded once again.

The meaning of "I love the twilight hours",
With peace our own as daily pressures fly,
This loving now enhances all my powers,
With godly gifts my heart cannot deny.

Valentine Oh Valentine

I will write you a play for this time and this age,
I will set it in scenes on a grandiose stage,
With actors who strut and who fake and who cry,
With never a truth to be heard with the lie.

I will sing you a love song to set the world free,
A love song to act as my advocate's plea,
A love song to ring round the stars and the moon,
And to whisper of loves that have ended too soon.

Let me spin you a story a web of deceit,
Let me tell how the mighty have tasted defeat,
And when you have felt me bite deep to the bone,
Let me shake your hand empty and leave you alone.

For this is the love for this time and this age,
And why I must chronicle vitriol rage,
For we anger the angels when fearless we tread,
On the hopes of the living and peace of the dead.

They say love of money belies love of god,
But what will it matter when under the sod,
When the stones in the churchyard recording our powers,
Are all that are left of our days and our hours.

So kindle a fire in one true lover's heart,
Reach out, your soul naked, and make a new start,
Take hold of your destiny make it a prize,
And empty your pockets of panic and lies.

I have loved as a liar and lied into love,
And let my mendacity fit like a glove,
I have written seduction and counted my gold,
But have not known of wisdom until I am old.

For the sweet consolation, the ties that held fast,
When the ship of my life came to harbour at last,
When the passions were stilled in a deep flowing tide,
That brought home my longings and emptied my pride.

God knows me a sinner, if god there may be,
But something inside me is setting me free,
Though the fires still burn they are warmth to my soul,
And my love is my buttressing making me whole.

Though never a prophet and never a sage,
I have played out my act on the grandiose stage,
I have prayed for gods laughter and acted the clown,
As I charged like the cavalry cutting men down.

But I look to forgiveness in one woman's eyes,
Who has levelled my pride and my mountain of lies,
Who has offered me mercy without want or greed,
And given me harvest from sanctuaries seed.

And so to my blessing if blessing I may,
A poor mans beatitude fit for the day,
Let love be a flame that burns bright though your years,
Dispelling all darkness and stifling fears.

When I Am Gone

When I am just a memory,
Don't call to me in the heat of day,
But seek me out in the evening mist,
A shadow where we used to stray.

And do not cry when I am gone,
For tears were never you and I,
I loved you then, I love you now,
Lost though I be, I never die.

For day by day this world will turn,
Sweet consolation to mankind,
And we will be a part of all,
Though not a trace is left behind.

A form of words in a broken rhyme,
A trace of blood in the living street,
When all that's gentle all that's fine,
Is kirtled by the winding sheet.

In kindness sometimes think of me,
Who never sought for wealth or fame,
Then love and I will ever love,
While ever love you speak my name.

Woman

She is not fair,
Not like a blossom kissed by dew,
But soft upon the care worn soul,
And warm to me and ever true.

She is not kind,
Where kindness bides is often pain,
She holds me and the world is new,
And I am young and free again.

She is not giving,
But in her gift is all I seek,
She comforts me through all my days,
And proves my strength when I am weak.

She is not constant,
Where constancy is but a jail,
Where love abides no need for chains,
No need to claim, no chance to fail.

She is not gentle,
But burns me in exquisite flame,
And yet I own she owns my heart,
Who has my love and has my name.

A Yorkshire Living

A Child of 1944

The world itself was crying,
When I came to birth in tears,
And I have cried with pain and joy,
Throughout the flowing years.

At school I knew injustice,
And escape in a written rhyme,
A hope in the hope of reason,
And a faith in the balm of time.

Where haste made me unready,
The haste just bought me shame,
When lust for another burned me,
As nameless took my name.

The winds blew chill when father died,
Though I never felt alone,
But when my mother passed away,
They froze me to the bone.

And in that tortured ending,
When death had passed me by,
I found a new beginning,
And solace in a sigh.

For I saw as the days were running,
By decade and by age,
That life became a sonnet,
Of passions love and rage.

So what could I ask from the future,
What more could I seek than I own,
The love in the love of a woman,
The chance of a chance to atone.

So faced with a new beginning,
Of lifetime love or year,
I know this world unchanging,
Still turns with hope and fear.

That verses yet unwritten,
And children yet unborn,
Will prove ten thousand thousand years,
Are just another dawn.

When all that we are is forgotten,
When the final sun has set,
And the gods sing songs of triumph,
Will they whisper of our regret.

A Fifties Childhood

Walk to school by field and hedgerow,
Cap pulled down against the rain,
Eating rhubarb dipped in sugar,
Eke the rations out again.

Boxy cars with side-valve engines,
Temperamental at their best,
Petrol one and nine a gallon,
No real need to pass a test.

Fridges proffered by the gas board,
Gas flames generating ice,
Only twelve inch television,
Just a black and white device.

See the King on 'Pathe' newsreels,
Mr Churchill with cigar,
Children's flicks all in for fourpence,
Humphrey Bogart 'what a star'.

On the tram to old Leeds market,
Traders crying out their wares,
Home again in smog and darkness,
Policemen lead with carbide flares.

Friends who never knew their fathers,
Bought it in the D day push,
Queues outside the better bakers,
Almost trampled in the crush.

Home made jams and cloudy honey,
Home cured bacon salty dry,
Stately sermons on a Sunday,
Better not to steal or lie.

Touch your forelock to the parson,
God is represented here,
No salvation just religion,
State support and sanctioned fear.

Bicycle through empty byways,
Catching bullheads in the stream,
Luxemburg till seven thirty,
Then to bed and time to dream.

Companionship unique and worthy,
Scuffing knees and breaking bones,
Truer friends I never wanted,
Memories like shattered stones.

Smallpox and the fear of conflict,
Watch the commies Stalin's crew,
Mother said that things are better,
There's a better life for you.

But all in all that life was gentle,
Hazy days of sweet content,
Lazy days that were my growing,
Coins of childhood safely spent.

Walk the fields of recollection,
Take the tram down memory lane,
All of yesterdays tomorrows,
Comforting the heart and brain.

A July Evening

As quiet steals upon the hill,
And daily clamours from you fly,
Of gentle twilight seek your fill,
And round you wrap a warm July.

Where in the meadows hares at sport,
Snatch at a sound and then are gone,
When all your troubles come to naught,
As natures many blend to one.

Where streams reflect the evening star,
And hold its light when all is still,
Should nothing hurt and nothing jar,
And nothing stay creations will.

When blue black night caresses all,
And scented air fills every glade,
Who can resist the ancient call,
Of which a summer night is made.

A Sixties Adolescence

Just fourteen and not yet shaving,
Awkward at the youth club dance,
Older girls in floral dresses,
Knowing that I had no chance.

Harder grind at daytime lessons,
Can't do French its such a bore,
English homework that's a pleasure,
Simple signs of what's in store.

Khrushchev settled in the Kremlin,
Shadows of the mushroom cloud,
Batten down the A-Bomb shelter,
Play the music long and loud.

On to college wine and cider,
Campus pleasures through the night,
Flirting at a student demo,
Posers for the greater fight.

Certain now I'd missed the call up,
National Service not for me,
Plan for life and not for dying,
Live for now not history.

Buy a Norton motorcycle,
Featherbedded in its frame,
BSA's no competition,
AJS are much the same.

Freedom of the open highway,
Pocket money takes you far,
Feel the speed that sets blood coursing,
Burn the road and touch the star.

First real love, a wayward pleasure,
Lustful longings quite sublime,
Days to dream and endless evenings,
Days of wonder, endless time.

Twenty now and quite immortal,
Twenty now both sure and proud,
Jet black hair and six foot something,
Don't I stand out from the crowd?

Evenings in the city nightclubs,
Waiting for the slower dance,
Lovely girls in short tight dressers,
Knowing I have every chance.

Weekday mornings in the office,
Starting on the corporate climb,
Bite your lip and mind the bosses,
Watching clocks and wasting time.

Sell at last the motorcycle,
Buy a car with room for two,
Better be a man in manhood,
That's the proper thing to do.

So that was my adolescence,
Wild and witty, fast and free,
Taught me all that is my being,
Told in all what life should be.

A Summer Goodbye

We had spoken only for moments,
Of her home and the life that she led,
Now I came with a clamour of others,
To find her cold, lonely and dead.

We had needed to force an entry,
With tools better made for repair,
Dispassionate strangers who saw her,
With just enough feelings to care.

We summoned the police and the medics,
And they did what they do by the book,
As the small children gathered to question,
And the neighbours all gathered to look.

Yet I think and I puzzle and wonder,
Over what had occurred in that night?
Where a light had burned on in the darkness,
And a life force had taken to flight.

There was nothing of fear, nothing bitter,
In the sad silent form in the chair,
And nothing to break on the stillness,
Or move in the soft fetid air.

As strangers we gazed on a stranger,
While we did all that had to be done,
But we found that mortality touched us,
As we left in the bright summer sun.

A Village Memorial Not Far From Home

I stand and look at what is written here,
An age has passed and still the letters cry,
For men who left with precious hope and pride,
A fading list of those who went to die.

The names repeat and then repeat again,
Familial but every one alone,
Cold words that cypher sacrifice and pain,
Hard cut upon the sharp and polished stone,

These lost who once had honour, life and breath
Now heroes all remembered at the last,
As prisoners of this legends proud decree,
These soldiers of a soon forgotten past.

They fell as heavens treasure to the ground,
And this may be their only trace and mark,
I cannot know the best of what they were,
These words have left us not a single spark.

So read at least one name and speak it loud,
To give them breath and one more living day,
They gave us all of more than we can know,
Who are forever prized and precious clay.

Bullocks

There are bullocks in the meadow,
Moving coarsely through the mist,
Where stately ladies used to walk,
The proud parade, the numbered list,

They took me to my childhood,
To a very different place,
When I was just a bullock,
In a different time and space.

And this my bullock status,
Made me different as I grazed,
A man-child in a harem,
To be cherished and amazed.

Not that the cows were always still,
And cowards do survive,
The goring horn is sharp as steel,
Among the strong when you are five.

Yet all my life I ride their backs,
The ghostly and the graven few,
Some whom I loved and those I feared,
And those I wish I never knew.

A bullock yes, both coarse and gauche,
Still quite surprised by female kind,
Not learning much but gaining time,
My hope to come, my past behind.

What purpose has a bullock then,
What better cause, what test of fate,
To eat the grass and mulch the field,
And end up on the dinner plate.

But if it comes that I am served,
On some round platter at the feast,
Perhaps I will fulfil the cause,
As carcase of the winning beast.

Analogies and wistful rhymes,
Can open windows, paint and draw,
This bullock that was in my child,
Is conjuring and nothing more.

But in this magic black and white,
Emasculation is the key,
Behold the child, Behold the man,
That woman made but did not free.

Buttercup

We pluck the blossom from the lawn,
Gold doubloons from an emerald sward,
And in this labour I can see,
No great release and no reward.

This flush of colour bright and strong,
A weed set down in ordered space,
A lock upon the gate of heaven,
A jewel in a common place.

And yet this complex complete form,
Holds all the truth that I would be,
Not ordered, fettered line on line,
But roaming riot bold and free.

For down the meadow past the wall,
In wild profusion lost to measure,
In seed and blossom root and stem,
This golden hoard is nature's treasure.

So as we stoop and bow again,
This contradiction to confound,
I honour now this yellow flower,
That glorifies the precious ground.

Carrion Spring

I saw amid the lambs at play,
One sleeping in the haze,
But something in that still repose,
Caused me to stop and gaze.

I looked down at the silent form,
And saw the stain of death,
Vitality had ebbed away,
No life, no spark, no breath.

Here early spring was carrion,
Here promise all was done,
And nothing could be set aside,
Beneath the fading sun.

But then what does it matter,
In mankinds greater scheme,
Where lovers walk in rapture,
Where poets sit and dream.

For who gives absolution,
When the people live in dread,
And God alone is comfort,
For the living and the dead.

Chain Ringing

They say in old Byzantium there hung a bell of gold,
It swung beneath the library dome to summon young and old,
A burnished thing both mighty wrought and stunning to the eye,
Whose sonorous note caressed the tower and echoed out the sky.

But golden bells are gilded waste their glory little worth,
Too precious and too soft at heart to clamour on the earth,
The brightest metal brought to base too dull for ringing true,
But something in the ring of bells sets ringing me and you.

An iron bell will clatter clang and set your ears to smart,
No gentle form this clappered fiend will cut you to the heart,
No blessing knell for Christendom from this unholy sprite,
That wrecks the halls of solitude and breaks the rest of night.

Some mighty bells like Ben and Tom we name as big or great,
With Sounding Michael resonant to steer the ship of state,
For in both rhyme and rhapsody we laud their mighty call,
As if the very voice of god was speaking to us all.

What founders art what founders wit first gave these titans life,
What alchemy of molten bronze brought music from the strife,
What was it there in Whitechapel that made base metal sing,
And gave to us a march through time with every measured ring.

And still they are calling out to me from their eyrie of infinite dread,
Like a surfeit of Sunday sermons they have drawn me awake from my bed,
They summon in anger cutting my soul and I hear as they render the sky,
An angelus sounding the passing of years, the accusers my life can't deny.

But there's joy in the ringing, laughter too, sadness and sorrow and pain,
Though bells have no feelings they mirror our moods and offer a mirrored refrain,
So always remember the sound of the bells may just be the call to the feast,
As clamouring bells that have heralded war will tell when the battle has ceased.

One day the bells will be ringing for me but I hope they will toll with mirth,
Such bells have swung for me happily through all my days on earth,
They have led me to knowledge, counted my hours, serving me more than well,
And if I must sing in the eons to come let me sing with the song of the bell.

Commonality

I had this conversation with the mother of my spouse,
And viewed the garden that she tends to gentrify the house,
We came to the conclusion that we never would agree,
About the brave and various forms that nature gives for free.

There's glory in the chaos of the wild and wanton things,
The greenfinch in the hedgerow the buzzing wasp that stings,
The burdock and the nettle stems that green the pastures edge,
The reeds within the flowing beck, the meadowsweet and sedge.

Some take delight in butterflies, in bats and martin's flight,
In fallen pellets near the trees where owls have come at night,
The crane flies even have their place in rounding nature's plan,
A chaos not contaminate by all the wit of man.

And yet we need our order and our order binds the space,
No corner for the daisies in a green but perfect place,
No sanctuary for buttercups or rosebays stunning tower,
No kind collective of the fields protecting bird and flower.

And so I raise my cause-celebre, my passion in the grass,
A little thing a seasons hope but one I'll not let pass,
For out there in profusion is a treasure bright as gold,
That cheered me as little child, and comforts now I'm old.

Pernicious and perennial, a pest of baser birth,
Expunged from better company and poisoned from the earth,
Dug up and scarred and scarified, dissected dried and burned,
She still returns to haunt the land untroubled and unlearned.

I've seen her on the mountaintops of distant foreign lands,
And bordering the ocean in the ever-shifting sands,
The desert edges know her touch and welcome her embrace,
And in the very sunlight is the beauty of her face.

For in her commonality she blesses town and vale,
No light beneath a bushel here, no candle burning pale,
Just burning summers bright and brave and hope and honey sweet,
A miser's treasure for us all set free beneath our feet.

And what would be in winters end without her first full flush,
What else can conjure Pan's wild tune so profligate and lush?
What else can stir the simple soul and raise our eyes to god,
Than she who springs eternal new from every vacant sod.

And so my commendation and my honouring and peace,
My comfort, consolation, benediction and release,
I gaze out of my window and pour blessings on the hour,
When I behold the glories of the dandelion flower.

Consanguinity

What can I say, in testament, in foolishness of word and wit,
The tales men tell walk crooked and distorted down the years,
This creature born like others both gifted and deprived,
A prisoner in constant war acquitted by his tears.

We make mistakes, we fret and strive, in anger and regret,
We think we love till love departs and leaves us all alone,
The wraith we call our own career is fragile as the mist,
Depositing our hopes and dreams as epitaphs on stone.

But still we all march forward while begetting faith and will,
The army of the common man processed in endless stream,
The child of Eve and Adam forging shackles for his kind,
While god remains the spark of hope to sanctify the dream.

The children of my childrens child may never know my name,
But they will know how well I loved though all the ages fly,
The blood that is within them will shout the truth again,
And they will own the heart of me before their turn to die.

When I am called to heavens gate, to offer up my soul,
I then will be an empty song, some melody with sad refrains,
I leave behind in all my kin some lingered sound of all that was,
And I will be what I must be, a mighty ghost within their veins.

Crucible

I read that Arthur Miller died,
The words full flowed with conscious praise,
A panegyric for the man,
A warm reflection on his days.

His life like others bitter sweet,
Was woven in the words they spun,
Remembering the myth and man,
Concluding, closing all he'd done.

What privilege to spin each thought,
No matter what the critics say,
What if your line of labours love,
Is kindling for another day.

What sweet release to work your wit,
To challenge wisdom and provoke,
To build a tower to lift the mind,
Yet hide beneath a mask and cloak.

With unspent passions we inscribe,
And dive into a hidden pool,
Arising sometime truly blessed,
And sometime just a sodden fool.

I met a man some years ago,
A journalist, a cynics friend,
Who pounded words for paltry pence,
Yet knew the power to break and mend.

He taught me this if nothing more,
You write the window to your heart,
And that same pen that stains the hand,
Can rend the loving soul apart.

I sit here waiting for the dawn,
Another day in which to learn,
A sabbath for the inmost eye,
Another fire in which to burn.

So deep into the melting pot,
I cast my rune and throw my rhyme,
The window opens once again,
Displaying all our little time.

For in the end if all these words,
Have kindled just the smallest flame,
What matter if the gods decree,
That no one ever knows my name.

For David

I knew a man called David,
And David was a Jew,
And only in my nightmares
Could I share what he went through.

They took him from the ghetto,
They put him on the train,
They tore him from a mother,
He would never see again.

He was clinging to his sister,
Who simply cried and cried,
And in the crush he never knew,
The moment that she died.

Then in the camp he shovelled earth,
To cover up the dead,
And no-one came to comfort him,
Humanity had fled.

And through all this no bitterness,
No rage at god or man,
For having no contempt at all,
He saw the greater plan.

Old when I first knew him,
Though not aged by the years,
He treated me with kindness
And understood my fears,

> For marked like a beast and numbered,
> He had found a way to live,
> He taught me how to honour life,
> And taught me to forgive.

For David Salinski who died in poverty but as a very rich man.

Dog Food.

I'll set the scene 'the slaughter house'
The noise, the smell, the blood, the flies,
And in this reek I walked and woke,
To see where all compassion dies.

And in a pen, alone aloof,
A great old bull a mighty mound,
Who stood and watched and waited death,
But offered not a single sound.

This once proud heap, this thing of flesh,
Had been a king among his kind,
But here alone with lowered head,
Wide empty eyes and emptied mind.

My soul told him to strike and fight,
To die with pride, to rave and rage,
And stand against the will of men,
Who brought him to this bitter cage.

They killed him while I stood and watched,
Just fit for dog food I was told,
Will this be me I contemplate,
When I am weak, when I am old.

For fifty years he's touched my heart,
A beast that showed a way to truth,
Who helped me find a way to live,
But brought an end to treasured youth.

Exaltation

A dog they say can have no soul,
While priests and prelates spirits soar,
But are the crosier and the alb,
More comfort than a proffered paw.

A fox is cunning owls are wise,
An eagles eye is always clear,
The wolf is haunting in the night,
The lark is hope, the raven fear.

We make assumptions day by day,
Experience to no avail,
We poison clover in the lawn,
And cast away the wandering snail.

Yet nature sets each in its place,
A greater wisdom to impart,
If god there is then he must know,
That hope imbues the smallest heart.

For if dogs pine is this not love,
With souls not sanctified by grace,
And are snails in the lettuce patch,
Our equal in their time and place.

I contemplate and offer this,
Embracing what my mind can hold,
Are we all shepherds of this world,
Or keepers of a crumbling fold.

So recognise all life is kin,
To hold with love and raging calm,
Then fill all hope with all desire,
And want for time to do no harm.

Harvest Home

The sunset found the harvester still hungry for the corn,
The rabbits in the hedgerow were waiting for the dawn,
The clouds that ran the heavens had gained a distant glow,
And I was doing nothing with nowhere new to go.

The rooks were calling windward as their treasure drifted by,
As black as broken promises beneath a fading sky,
When quickly I was taken by the spirit in it all,
As I wandered in this garden as a man before the fall.

Where heaps of grain are pennies on a bankers yellow tray,
And gold is all but sunrise on another perfect day,
When the oak tree in the forest is the beam within my eye,
And all the truth in nature is the pattern of a lie.

Some say that god is watching from a mystic hidden place,
But I have yet no concept of his wisdom or his face,
If compassion then can hold me in the everlasting arms,
What need have I to contemplate this world and all its charms?

This harvest then is labour where a man might break his back,
The rabbits a pernicious pest on every path and track,
The rooks and thieving magpies bring a plague upon the earth,
And nature's rage is architect to strange and bitter mirth.

But hope can spring eternal from the beating of a heart,
From the laughter of a child of man eternity can start,
For when love is all fulfilling it will set this world to right,
And what was ever darkness will be bright and endless light.

Hawk

I have seen the wild red kite, as thunder in the air,
Ten thousand years upon the wind, unheeded, without care,
And ageless as the towering cliff it wrote its song to me,
As timeless as a flowing stream it spoke of what must be.

For the hawk still has its presence though it hides a broken wing,
And the gods would still have glory should the angels never sing,
When man is in his prime and pride the tower is built on sand,
While monarchies and majesties shall terrorise the land.

For without a trace of anger we send brothers to the fray,
And the swords we make from ploughshares are sufficient for the day,
What we give we give for pleasure though we reap in bitter fields,
And offer for the holocaust a foe that never yields.

But the fleece is always golden and the wind is always fair,
For the maiden in the meadow must have breezes in her hair,
While moonlight sleeps on silver hills sweet grace is close at hand,
And muses borne of ancient days cry gentle through the land.

Yet all the while the hawks still soar as watchers on the plain,
As hawks have watched ten thousand years and ever will again,
But I bide here to sit and write and watch with inner eyes,
And hide myself inside my soul to flatter the world with lies.

I Quite Like Blackbirds

I see the blackbirds fighting for the pickings on the lawn,
Where one will strut victorious the other leaves forlorn.
The robins not much better are calling from the briar,
And pout with self-importance with a plumage red as fire.

At night I hear the dog fox as he calls out to his mate,
A cry from the primeval fog to which I can relate,
The frog croaks in the reed-bed when the spawning time is near,
While pheasants flaunt their colours as the mists begin to clear.

The sexual imperative will drive the species on,
As was with all the dinosaurs before they all were gone,
The rutting stag is not alone when viewed with sober mind,
As fire imbues the stir of lust within the watching hind.

But all of this is animal for we who with gods trust,
Have seen the path to miracles and voided simple lust,
Have set the sons of Adam on the stairway to above,
And all alone have found the way to call our passions love.

And so we feel compassion that can hold the greater joy,
A winding sheet to knot the heart and bind a girl and boy,
The closeness that brings sacrifice transcending our desire,
That makes the worker in the field twice worthy of his hire.

But I have viewed corruption where the others see no blame,
What David was to Jonathan may have another name,
When David sought Uria's death it spoke of deeper powers,
The face of god not turned away in those his darkest hours.

And so I question what and why and even which and when,
What is this darker side of love this blessed curse of men,
We take the life of others as a final act of grace,
But fail to see the mirrored smile that stares us in the face.

We trust to one another just to see each other fail,
The cross of life, the hammer blow, another piercing nail,
We plead to gods when nature deals her worst in any hand,
And hoard our paltry pennies when the famine stalks the land.

The powered nation of our times declares 'In god we trust',
But questioning I dare to ask is this in love or lust,
For in the end are love and lust exchangeable for good,
And are they both like sin and salt embedded in the blood.

And so I leave these questions and these riddles for our time,
Are we much more than faulted things that shadow the sublime?
And are we more than rutting stags or robins in the briar?
And have we moved from them to now by blessing or desire

March

I am the Lion of winter,
And I rage at the dawning of light,
My teeth are the ice in the north wind,
My mane is the mist of the night.

I come with a roar in the forest,
And I render the branch and the bough,
I honour the storm like a brother,
And we gather a harvest now.

My tears set the wild rivers flowing,
As I thunder my call from the sky,
My talons cut deep in the lightning sweep,
For the lion of winter must die.

For I am the lamb in the meadow,
And the blossom that glows in the wood,
And I am the leaf in the hedgerow,
And a promise so long understood.

I must die to the glory of springtime,
I must die for the Lark and the Dove,
I must die to a rest in the sunlight,
I must die to the promise of love.

New Years Eve

At night I stood in the winter chill in the moonshadow stark and deep,
And looked at the village soft and warm safely and soundly asleep,
The last year has ended its pleasure and pride and gone is the glory and pain,
And the wind that chills my heart and my soul has settled its ice on my brain.

For I wonder what will the new-year bring as we stride through its open gate,
And what will await us and what can we do as we deal with the follies of fate,
Can I alter the pattern of what went before, and walk on a far different road,
Or am I imprisoned by all of my life and bearing a burdensome load.

For all our concerns we must take to the path that stretches away to our end,
And if it meanders then all to the good for surprises await round each bend,
For what then is life if the outcome is sure and all is quite certain and set,
No place for emotion and no place for love and no certain home for regret.

I have had years of plenty and sat at the feast and tasted the famine as well,

And what would be heaven unless I had walked through the gates
  of a personal hell,
To have loved and have hated is both meat and drink to the
  dutiful children of Eve,
And what is elation and what is success to the few who have not
  had to grieve.

I write and I ponder and ponder and write as the days and the
  decades slip by,
And as I grow older I prattle and rhyme and offer each reason a
  lie,
But I still wake in wonder and wait for the light as dreamers have
  done for an age,
And know I'm the player of fanciful things who struts on this
  fabulous stage.

I was born in the forties and spoke to the old who told then of
  different days,
Some of them hard crushed by poverties claw but some of them
  times to amaze,
They told of the life when Victoria reigned in an empire where
  suns never set,
They told of the battles they told of the might but never once
  spoke of regret.

But we now must struggle to find a new place in a world that is
  shrunken and small,
With all of our politics oh so correct and the differences too close
  to call,
Where reasoned religion is cause to divide and kith and kin bicker
  and fret,
And it's better to hide from realities wrath and a man's bitter
  strivings forget.

But the gates yawning open, the path is so wide with a prospect to beckon me on,
And knowing of nothing I feel I must go where my fathers before me have gone,
Both the curse and the bounty of every new-year are willing me know of their charm,
And the bells that are tolling out time that is past are ringing in joy not alarm.

So I walk on in wonder with hope at my side like a pilgrim whose goals are in sight,
And with this companion in whom I must trust I must seek out the truth and the right,
Whatever awaits me I know at the last that something of me will transcend,
And what better epitaph can a man leave than he understood hope as a friend.

And should there be tears let them fall like the rain that ends in the sunniest day,
Let me be a potter that fashions new life from the basest and bitterest clay,
For if I take nothing from what I have learned but a truth that to love is sublime,
Then that will be everything, all that I need, from this year to the ending of time.

Newsprint

The bulwark of democracy,
Or so the media say,
But huff, puff and hyperbole,
More often seems the way.

Where spin is more important,
Than the simple truth or lie,
And judgements fit for Solomon,
Have silenced freedoms cry.

Where peers protest their innocence,
With perjured straightened face,
And honest men are pilloried,
And hounded to disgrace.

Where tabloid sheets corrupt the young,
And gossips still endure,
While all those not responsible,
Squeeze pennies from the poor.

Again I'm being cynical,
And that is no surprise,
This week I read the papers,
And was staggered by the lies.

Where quiet men are so distressed,
They cannot value life,
And words accomplish only this,
A widow from a wife.

Where frenzy follows every move,
As miscreants are freed,
And to sell the holy copy,
Is the true and blessed creed.

They tell us what we want to hear,
And fabricate the rest,
To move and then manipulate,
Damnation to the best,

But then like them I spin with words,
To calculate and sway,
And with the power of literature,
I push and prove my way.

A whore who bought a dictionary,
A mercenary of hype,
A priest of all corruption,
In the tyranny of type.

Ragged Beauty

I worked in the poorer quarter,
I saw much but knew little more,
I watched like the watchman waiting,
At the closed and the hard bolted door.

I suppose she had not turned forty,
But a century bore her down,
Beset by her truanting children,
In the slums of the shadowing town.

Perhaps she had been a beauty,
Perhaps she had danced until dawn,
But now she was older and empty,
In a dress that was dirty and torn.

My mind rushed to past lives and lovers,
When the world was a spectre of light,
As we laughed and we sang in the moonlight,
And the future was hopeful and bright.

It was chips and some scraps for her children,
Though she could have nothing at all,
No coins in her purse or her pocket,
And none there to answer her call.

And I with abundance ignored her,
Though it's true I had plenty to spare,
A plenty to do what I please with,
But not enough plenty to care.

And I know when I gaze from my window,
Onto sun-scented meadow and cott,
That there in the shadowing township,
Are realities better forgot.

For I will and I want to change nothing,
What I do will defend what I know,
And I have no reason to tear down one stone,
In the place where the ragged ones go.

And yet there is something inside me,
That orders my life to atone,
For a mother with truanting children,
Who is lost and so very alone.

Perhaps and perhaps and then maybe
I'll do something and nothing today,
For there's always the sun-scented meadow,
When these shadows have faded away.

Reflection

When as a child I wondered free,
To gaze at all there was to see,
And gather shrapnel pieces where,
The battery had cut the air,
To visit where the blast had shook,
The factory that bridged the brook,
And in the crater now a bog,
Play happily with friends and dog.

And with the prisoner long time back,
Who could not walk the railway track,
Without the ghostly shades of they,
That lay within the Burma clay,
This soldier young with aged mind,
Who closed the page and left behind,
The horror that he had to know,
And grief he could not bear to show.

And those who told of their good war,
And seemed to want for nothing more,
But I saw how their hands would shake,
And sometimes how a voice would break,
When eyes would stare into a day,
That years ago and far away,
Had turned some cards for death or pain,
Those cards they daily turn again.

And I have lived these many years,
And known my nations hopes and fears,
But I have never had to stand,
With just a rifle in my hand,
And know that I must kill or die,
And all my actions justify,
To those who come in years to be,
And may not cherish liberty.

My father's medals gather dust,
My shrapnel pieces turn to rust,
And I the man with locks of grey,
Can shake my head and turn away,
But still with gratitude can smile,
Or yet reflect some little while,
When all is said and all is done,
There is no peace beneath the sun.

Resolutions

Not faint or fool to harsh regret,
No guilty feelings come to call,
The cards once dealt I seize and play,
And win or lose I love them all.

Contempt's contentment stills the soul,
As bitter herbs the palate pall,
But better still to crush the doubt,
And blame the serpent for the fall.

This tapestry we call our lives,
Is threadbare long before it's done,
The matchless turns to thin brocade,
And colours fade before the sun.

The penitential fast and feast,
Condemning all exalting few,
Feeds like coarse unleavened bread,
Where heavens manna falls like dew.

Aquinas, Luther and the rest,
Reformers heretics or worse,
In prayer both blessed and sanctified,
Or condemned coldly with a curse.

Yet they would say they followed on,
In steps determined years before,
To shadow one who only served,
And opened wide redemptions door.

Tempted they say for forty days,
To panoplies of world delight,
To power beyond a tyrants dreams,
Or bread to eat and rest at night.

So once again and every year,
My challenge set, the cure to take,
To shrive and purge the intellect,
And corporal cause to clean or break.

I last on average half a week!
The devil has me in his claw,
This glutton wanting cake not bread,
And even finer wine to pour.

Not faint or fool to harsh regret,
The guilt not racking bone and blood,
I comfort me in knowing this,
My penitence will do no good.

But what I know may not be true,
And truth to ask what truth to trust,
When I like Popes and prelates all,
Will soon be so much scattered dust.

Some day my pride may bring me down,
One day some grace may bring me peace,
I wait for that beatitude,
When sacrifice will give release.

Rosaria Remembered

She had beaten and burned and chained me,
Till the iron of my manhood was cast,
And as I was a part of her future,
She is mightily part of my past.

When she died there were scores to be settled,
But revenge is not sweet on the dead,
By the sad common pit where they laid her,
I wept for the words never said.

As I cried and I asked for forgiveness,
For the times when I failed to forgive,
In that moment I held that I knew her,
And in hers was the life that I live.

In remembrance story and fable,
Passed down in familial round,
She is living again in her pleasures,
Resting cold in the sanctified ground.

I wish I believed in a heaven,
Still I'm glad I acknowledge no hell,
Though an object of pain for her passion,
It is only of love that I tell.

For sorrow and pain have an ending,
As will anger and passion and lust,
And for what will we all be remembered,
When we all are but ashes and dust.

So I seek for the true reformation,
In the blood of my heart and my hand,
And the peace in the true contemplation,
That the lovers of love understand.

When I ask in my turn for forgiveness,
When the rigours of life are all past,
May my soul be at rest and remembered,
For the haven I came to at last.

In remembrance of my Grandmother 'Rosaria Facchini'

Scraps

Answer me spirit I said to the shade,
Tell me of things that are waiting to be,
What now awaits in the years that will come,
And what from the shadows is following me.

What of this world that my heart holds so dear,
What of my hopes of my dreams and my fears,
Will I have joy that will pleasure my soul,
And will I know pain in the valley of tears.

What can I change while my eyes cannot see,
Stygian darkness and bright blinding light,
First to the footpath and first to the stile,
With no one to tell me of which way is right.

Storms on the mountain and rain in the vale,
Locked in my prison I reach for the key,
Life has encompassed me bound me in chains,
But fortune and learning are setting me free.

Age has not taught me, I drift through my days,
But scraps from life's table are intellects food,
Wisdom is caught in the net of the mind,
Where all must be wholesome and nothing is crude.

And so down the days and the months and the years,
For the scraps from life's table we bicker and fight,
The books and papers are scoured and scanned,
We read in with horror and hear with delight.

There are books of great learning and heretic tomes,
And words of great enmity sounding the drum,
But knowing and reading I'm forced to conclude,
That nothing in knowledge can tell what's to come.

So humour me spirit and look with my mind,
Look deep in my soul and see men with my eyes,
See why I can love with both passion and pride,
But find it so easy to hate and despise.

So take to the weigh-scales the burden I bear,
The fears of the cynic the hopes of a fool,
The dreams of a child and the words of a whore,
The mercy of god and the wit of a mule.

And so to the footpath and so to the stile,
For though I may stumble life beckons me on,
The years are for me and for me to possess,
Till the scraps from their table are eaten and gone.

Shambles

It was early in the morning on a rain swept city road,
That I saw an old and older man hard burdened by his load,
His hair was tousled wired grey beneath a shapeless cap,
And all this world for all his life had held him like a trap.

Surprised at my reaction, the contempt that flooded in,
This thing of flesh, humanity, our human race to win,
Was I then so superior that I could stand aside,
And designate my own success as anchor for my pride.

I saw that he was sodden from his coat down to the bone,
A shambling world of emptiness, crushed, broken and alone,
But then I felt a sadness for this wretched wreck and me,
For there in his perception were the things I could not see.

How great would be his story and how wonderful his ways,
How spirited his journeys and how marvellous his days,
What wisdom circles in his mind with every onward tread,
What loss will compass all the world when he is cold and dead?

I watched him in the mirror as I slowly drove on by,
Another tramp, another day, another rain filled sky,
And shuddered as I realised we two were of an age,
A pair of fading actors on an ever changing stage.

Will what I leave be greater, will I sweeten bitter tears,
A blessing in the memory that casts aside all fears?
And place love as my epitaph in hope and heart and mind,
Or shamble into nothingness with not a glance behind?

SCOTT HALL ROAD LEEDS. 7.00am February 22nd 2001

Stones

The roads we take have many ways,
And all are strewn with builder's stone,
I walk and gather day by day,
Sometimes with love, sometimes alone.

What treasure must a wanderer store,
Where stone is heavy, laughter light,
No mason's hoard can lift the soul,
Or guide me home if love takes fright.

I trust and mix these bonds of life,
With mortar that cements the years,
I offer stone for every course,
And wet the trowel with my tears.

Perhaps I build without the plan,
Creating without wit or scheme,
And seeing ramparts without end,
I raise the towers of a dream,

For I would make from all my stones,
No monument no hand wrought ridge,
And from my life no prison walls,
But from my love an ageless bridge.

Swallows on Whitestone Hills

I was high on the hills over Settle,
The day that the swallows returned,
The haze on the whitestone shimmered,
And the sun in the heavens burned.

The bleating of lambs was a chorus,
To the new summer song on the air,
For god was at ease in his glory,
And I was a stranger to care.

I was free as the wind on the hillside,
With hands that could hold and caress,
Free to walk down a path to my lover,
And be offered a reason to bless.

For mine is the mind of a poet,
Seeking grace in the eyes of a friend,
Reaching out to the stars for a moment,
Being lost in a love without end.

Though I know and I feel I am mortal,
I am lifted beyond even truth,
For lost as I am in another,
My ageing has given me youth.

Swansong

Full thirty-five in number they made an eerie sight,
Wild swans like ghosts all wing on wing,
Pale horses from the night,
And through the mist a silent song came crying down the years,
An end to all that was to be,
A sacrament of tears.

Rejoice then for submission now will bring an end to pain,
And love will never touch a hand,
Nor kiss the lips again,
The cold that soon caresses life in all consuming fire,
While gods cry out to emptiness,
The torch is at the pyre.

But still the swans fly onward as souls toward the sun,
Where in the light perpetual,
All earthly toil is done,
Where passions unrequited are sanctified and blessed,
And children that were never born,
Lead parents to their rest.

Gods grace, a heart, the crashing sea, all motion never still,
A turning world an endless age,
The majesty of will,
To live with strength and fortitude with tragedy and pride,
And know that as mankind lives on,
No man has ever died.

In Memory Of My Godfather Joe Facchini

Tadpoles in a Jar.

I very nearly killed the child,
The child with tadpoles in a jar,
Whose dog was just a breath away,
Who walked beneath a different star.

This son of man with raven hair,
Who offered life a faulted grin,
And emptied books like whiskey jars,
For words to shout above the din.

I watched him then when aged just ten,
He cast his faith in god away,
And strew with stones the upward path,
That leads to where he is today.

I very nearly killed the child,
When placed ambition made him mean,
While others set the honey trap,
Like actors in his painted scene.

A fretful fool who wanted hope,
When hope was only callow style,
Who danced as satyrs pulled the strings,
And walked alone his pilgrims mile.

I watched him then at twenty five,
Forget his sense and then comply,
To have and lose the kind of love,
That made his muse a bitter lie.

I very nearly killed the child,
When life laid bare a crooked road,
Where gods foretold an early end,
The time to cast away the load.

No faulted grin to ease the way,
With life endangered wracked with fear,
With lifelessness a breath away,
The pilgrims staff and satyrs tear.

I watched him then at fifty some,
Grasp at a feather, strive to win,
And self forgiving find his hope,
In what was seen as greater sin.

I very nearly killed the child,
But now instead I set him free,
The jar of tadpoles in my hand,
Is proof at last the child is me.

The Angelus in Thornton

At noon and six it rends the air,
And strangers stop to wonder where,
While watch is checked and clocks are read,
Or yet a silent prayer is said,
The angelus in Thornton.

While black clad clerics hurry by,
The clangour reaches to the sky,
Still cattle do not cease to graze,
Amidst the meadows summer haze,
The angelus in Thornton.

And did it sound five hundred years,
Of quiet hope and humble tears,
And cry from abbey steeple dumb,
Sub malleus monasterium,
The angelus in Thornton.

The cat that stalks the churchyard stones,
Steps silent over dust and bones,
Of those who do not hear the knell,
As David Miller Rings the bell,
The angelus in Thornton.

*In memory of my friend Fr Francis Pepper
and of David Miller 'sometime Br Nicholas of Pluscarden Abbey'.*

The Melody of May

May, the month of brides and blossom,
Spring begins her first flood flush,
Nature bursts like bright balloons,
Songbirds sing in every bush.

Clouds scud by with rain forgotten,
Days speed longer nights are clear,
Gentle thoughts and gentle daydreams,
Gentle winds to warm and cheer.

In the fields the grass is growing
Crops are sprouting fresh and green,
Life has burgeoned filled the woodland,
All is giving, nothing mean.

Life around me full and wondrous,
Life around me loud and new,
Spilled like sunlight from the heavens,
Early mist and crystal dew.

Yet we must improve on nature,
Spray the meadow boost the yield,
Kill the wildflowers in the margins,
Strike the rabbits from the field.

Steal a march on moth and cranefly,
Rape the hedgerows with the flail,
Line the ditch with pipes of plastic,
Leave behind no grub or snail.

Make up songs to feed our neighbours,
Dream of food on every plate,
Count the cost in reams and reasons,
Live the love of what we hate.

I'm to blame and don't I know it,
Mother Nature has her price,
Cutting costs I will destroy her,
End up paying more than twice.

Nations penny-pinch the needy,
Supermarkets drive cost down,
Rural idylls count for nothing,
Feeding the rapacious town.

Still I see the fields in fallow,
Hear the chorus in the dawn,
May the month of brides and blossom,
Makes me just a touch forlorn.

The Star and the Crescent Moon

The chimneys cast long shadows,
And the smoke is a bitter shroud,
But the phoenix from the human ash,
Flies powerful and proud.

The home for the diaspora,
The nation once returned,
And who could fail to understand,
When millions have burned.

And yet, and yet the blood still cries,
And why we ask and why,
Can we assess when truth is told,
Or yet discern the lie.

For in our art and literature,
And in our media too,
We praise the noble Arab,
And curse the grasping Jew.

Then in the blinding converse,
We hate the Muslim stand,
And laud the righteous Israelites,
Who occupy the land.

Of course it's all beyond me,
In my safe suburban street,
I never hear the sounds of war,
The tramp of soldiers feet.

My history does not include,
The camps of death and hate
Or looking at the land I owned,
Through someone's kibbutz gate

And so I let the others think,
The wise men and the just,
The statesmen and the generals
Who all of us can trust,

For how can it be dangerous,
For safe in England me,
If people in the middle-east,
Are neither safe nor free.

It can't affect the way we live
Or change the price of oil,
No chance of racial tension here,
No terrorists to foil.

No nail bombs blasting in our streets,
It couldn't happen here,
And why should folk with darker skins,
Give me some cause to fear.

But like the rest I'm worried,
When the leaders rant and rave,
And the land of milk and honey,
Is edged by a yawning grave.

The Summer of Sixty-two

I knew a girl with milk white skin,
With chastity like auburn hair,
Who I loved so wildly in the days,
When I was young and she was fair.

We walked in meadows fresh with dew,
To pluck the flowers where we dare,
And drag the moonlight from the sky,
When I was young and she was fair.

We whispered nothings to the winds,
And sang our songs without a care,
The spirits rising in our souls,
When I was young and she was fair.

And with this passions lust for life,
We baited dragons in their lair,
And fought to burn the castles down,
When I was young and she was fair.

And as we dreamed of myths and mist,
While others turned the backward stare,
We raised the gods to cuckolds then,
When I was young and she was fair.

For I was power and I was might,
The knight upon the winged mare,
With beaten armour, brightest steel,
When I was young and she was fair.

But fine reflections fade like fog,
As hopes will tumble to despair,
Just memory the wondrous days,
When I was young and she was fair.

The full bright hope of youthful dreams,
A candle bright, the lanterns glare,
The years diminished not at all,
When I was young and she was fair.

And now full sixty years and more,
I know her old and hard to bear,
I think of her and what we were,
When I was young and she was fair.

But consolation, Oh sweet life,
A harvest field without a tare,
I wish her blessings now as then,
When I was young and she was fair.

The Tailor

I saw a man of faultless dress,
In smart dark suit and formal tie,
Whose airs gave credence to the world,
His semblances a social lie.

An observation nothing more,
For mirrors show just what we are,
The dark reflection of ourselves,
The sepulchre with door ajar.

Cold comfort then when we are vain,
When rust corrupts and moths destroy,
Where pretty girls can spin the world,
And men make love a broken toy,

Oh churlish me who empties dreams,
And pleasures whimsy in each rhyme,
I seek to challenge and provoke,
To comment on my age and time.

I have my reasons, some profound,
They strike and shake and cut me down,
A masochistic trembling tide,
To make the strongest swimmer drown.

I wear my suit it fits me well,
An armour, helm and breastplate strong,
I am at once magnificent,
I am at once the sirens song.

So wear your clothes in colours bright,
Be bright as diamond, brazen bold,
And cut your cloth for everyman,
The winding sheet when you are old.

The Tiger And Tomorrow

I stood and I looked at the tiger,
While the tiger gazed back at me,
And I saw in his total disinterest,
That neither of us could be free.

He was caged in the best of surroundings,
He had food and the greatest of care,
There were plenty of paying admirers,
And the odour of total despair.

I was told he was born from a captive,
And this was the life that he knew,
His species was safe in this prison,
Here in liberties graveyard the zoo.

When we've killed all his kind who had freedom,
And preserved what is left in a cage,
What love will have flowed from our efforts,
What dangers will lie in their rage.

When gods hand is our preservation,
And what we preserve is our joy,
Then perhaps we will find consolation,
In what we have failed to destroy.

To Field Marshall Earl Haigh But Many Years Too Late.

Three hundred and six all dead all clay,
With none to shed a tear or mourn,
Taken away by the generals whim,
Tied to a stake and shot at dawn.

No gentle hand would write to tell,
Grieving mother child or wife,
Not slaughtered by some raging foe,
But regulations claimed his life.

What happened to these sons of men?
What fear or longing made them fail?
And would we even be as strong,
When facing warfare's bitter hail.

Field Marshall stare with sightless eyes,
Three hundred and six were yours to save,
Immortalised, set stern in bronze,
But rest not easy in your grave.

IN MEMORY OF THE 306 OFFICERS AND MEN
'MAINLY VOLUNTEERS' WHO WERE
SHOT AT DAWN FOR DESERTION OR COWARDICE
IN THE GREAT WAR 1914 - 1918

Villager

This village fits like an old warm coat,
The sweat of years in thread and weave,
A place that bides to call you home,
A place your heart could never leave.

Its well-worn paths are comfort clear,
When city streets have dulled the brain,
And comfort clear is every step,
That takes away the work-worn pain.

Familiar as my own right hand,
The hill and hedgerow, beck and ditch,
The ploughing fields that beckons life,
The gold in autumn deep and rich.

And from my window on the world,
Each day I see the rabbits play,
Not mindful of the waiting gun,
That comes to sweep the world away.

Not mindful of the many years,
That I have watched the seasons wane,
A perfect oak has matched my days,
As viewed beyond my windowpane.

And that tall tree has blessed the eyes,
Of those who sleep beneath the sod,
Who knew the same as I know now,
Who waited hope and watched for god.

So like a coat against the chill,
I wrap myself in lane and stream,
Where memories shadow every rest,
And sultry buttress every dream.

The light is fading as I write,
The collared doves feed by the mire,
This village is my cornerstone,
For refuge, home and hearth and fire.

What city could contain my heart,
While love and friendship here abide,
This trembling place is in my soul,
A truth my life has not denied.

Wanderlust

To walk the streets of Marrakech, the flaming deserts dune,
To see the domes of Istanbul beneath the Asian moon,
The dark creeks of the Amazon where hidden orchids grow,
To cross the green Sargasso where the sailors shouldn't go.

The pyramids at Giza by the ever-fertile Nile,
To sit beside the Tiber and to contemplate a while,
Then in the streets of Bethlehem and by the Western Wall,
To stare at other travellers and to wonder at it all.

And thinking from a distance of the valleys of my home,
What need have I of desert wind or minaret or dome?
For what of mighty rivers and what more of painted seas,
When prayers for home and honoured hills can bring me to my knees.

There's something in the rush of wind within an autumn sky,
And something in the crisp of frost the heart cannot deny,
A something in the winter snow that sets the seasons right,
Like starlight in a clearing sky that sanctifies the night.

Spring flowers in an endless swathe, a fortune at your feet,
The first fine flush of evergreen, the bitter and the sweet,
The waking wasp, the bumblebee, the cuckoo with his call,
And flowing full the burgeoning that is the all and all.

In summer grows for everyman the barley and the wheat,
While heaven spreads a banquet rare beneath the wanderers feet,
What god disposes man must glean and bring the harvest home,
To granaries in Egypt and to treasuries in Rome.

For even in my homesick ways I feel the wanderlust,
Full knowing that in home and hearth are pleasures I can trust,
Secure in thought that spring will burst while I'm in distant lands,
Full trusting in the harvest home without my helping hands.

I'll see them cutting sugarcane on some soft scented isle,
And as I watch the butterflies I'll turn to home and smile.
And thank god for the aeroplane, for jets and kerosene,
For travellers cheques and package deals and other things
    obscene.

For hire cars and border posts and cocktails by the sea,
And for the folk impoverished who wait on you and me,
For shantytowns the tourist boards keep neatly out of sight,
And doing well for commerce by not doing what is right.

This hand it has offended with each cheque that I have signed,
This world I have diminished and its people have maligned,
But still I can't resist them' not the pull of distant climes,
For after all, I am in all, a product of my times.

Wishing

There were voles in the rush bound banking,
There were sticklebacks deep in the flow,
There were dragonflies crossing my childhood,
In the place where my memories go.

The meadowsweet never grew taller,
Where the reedmace hid me from sight,
And I sang with the chorus of nature,
As I drank in the sweetness of night.

My dog was my constant companion,
He had grown with me teacher and friend,
We were life in a living abundance,
In a time and a space without end.

Now a factory stands where I wandered,
Where I learned of the brightest and best,
And a car park nudges the knotted oak,
Where I laid my old dog to rest.

So tell me that all this is progress,
When the rivers of spirit are lost,
Though we sit and we count up our money,
Will our children be counting the cost?

Years Ahead

I walk into a landscape without formula or form,
No winter and no springtime and no sun to keep me warm,
No history no failings and no faulted wish of men,
No end and no beginning with no wonder and no when.

Where promise is eternal and all sacrifice is vain,
Where love is just a platitude and substitute for pain,
Where gods submit to worthless prayer to ease a sinners plight,
And nations claim democracy as reason for the fight.

These corridors where I have trod are ancient as the sea,
Where conquest care and enmity combine to set men free,
When light eternal casts its beams on castle, hall and cott,
And all that's all of yesterday is better best forgot.

Yet steeped in hope I journey on the decades flying by,
With dreams to bolster faith and fear I abrogate the lie,
I kiss the lips of solitude retaining peace within,
And holding plenty in my hands I subjugate my sin.

The gate is open to my stride the path is clear ahead,
For what is past is chronicled and well and truly dead.
The books record and memory plays tricks with every word,
And wit concludes the symphony is base and barely heard.

And yet I seek to stride the path and seek to still endure,
Whatever ails whatever fails still certain of the cure,
Still holding fast to what is good in comfort and in pride,
And count the days in fleeting thoughts that cannot be denied.

Apportioned joy and justice are the measure of my span,
If peace abounds what failure here or pleasure in the plan,
What saint will sing my gloria, what witch will cast her spell,
What church bell peals exuberant or sounds the final knell.

Break wide the gate, the slavers chain, be wanton but be wise,
Stride forward into innocence and comforts cure despise,
The hand of god is waiting still whatever you perceive,
And faith alone denying faith is cause enough to grieve.

The light within the bushel is my lantern for the way,
The salt that savours every dish is potter to my clay,
The hope that walks beside me is companion for the road,
The cause that has ennobled me will help me bear my load.

For I will walk the road again and feel each rock and rut,
The prison gate forced open and the chapel bolted shut,
The light of love in misted eyes when rapture fills the soul,
A life of grace where mans desire can be entire and whole.

Silhouettes of a Yorkshire Skyline

I stood by the gilded minarets,
As an evening sun went down,
Amid the silks and satins,
Of a grimy northern town.

From the shade of an eastern temple,
In the eye of a different god,
I searched the hasty streets of gold,
Where weaver girls once trod.

Our nation is what we have made it,
In an age that we scarce understand,
Still wrapped in the cause of reason,
In a changing yet changeless land.

We close up the churches and chapels,
We melt down the lectern and bell,
And search for a new understanding,
In the stories the strangers will tell.

In the book we are born to be brothers,
With a yoke still not easy to bear,
But truth is the hope for our future,
When we suffer our children to dare.

Dewsbury 2006

No Argument With The Gods

A Penny for The Saints

The force of the tsunami passed over like its waves,
I hardly turned to contemplate the thousands in their graves,
The hard and hidden tragedies that made the headlines bold,
Caused in me no calm reflection and imbued no bitter cold.

Am I hardened by the ages by the sorrow and the strife,
Am I swamped by the enormity and untold loss of life,
While damage in the scheme of things that must be rated small,
Has all the dread capacity to injure and appal.

The old words said in charity the duty is to pray,
But I am with the Pharisee and look the other way,
A pound coin in a bucket is anathema in time,
And long reflected ignorance is all at once sublime.

To be born in parts of Africa is doubtless a mistake,
With greedy politicians who are always on the take,
No thoughtful man of substance would be born on foreign shores,
And better to be friend to friend than succour distant cause.

There's hope for xenophobia, there's hope for little me,
Care not at all for prisoners while I at least am free,
Why not start burning people when you've finished burning books,
And why not bar their entry just because of someone's looks.

I can't abide a foreigner unless he's serving food,
I will not learn his language and his customs are quite crude,
He comes from somewhere different and I can't abide his race,
And sometimes I'm affronted when he looks me in the face.

But in his pale reflection in his aspect and his gaze,
Is the concept of humanity, the prospect to amaze,
Perhaps if I could take his hand and find the way to talk,
He'd make my road to Jericho an easy path to walk.

But still they raise the spectre of the famine and the war,
The wolf will always have his fangs the hawk will have his claw,
The pound or two I give away will make me feel at ease,
While someone else a world away is broken to his knees.

So dig deep in the pocket and give of what you can,
Remembering that what you do supports your fellow man,
As long as he's content to live on some far distant shore,
And doesn't want to move his kids into the house next door.

So vote for little Englanders support the status quo,
There's always somewhere, somewhere else for someone else to go,
But while we man the barricades and build the walls of clay,
We wait the great Tsunami that will sweep us all away.

A Road to Freedom.

I found my way on the road to freedom,
Littered with the songs of strife,
Searching for the sense and reason,
In a dark and bitter life.

Love was just a faulted echo,
Driven on by bitter gales,
Kindness walked behind me weary,
Step by step as courage fails.

Mystics told of stolen pleasure,
Solitude was true remorse,
Danger now in all my passion,
Life to death had run its course.

Then a light a brilliant splendour,
Liberty to hold and bless,
Kindly gentle and forgiving,
Folds me in forgetfulness.

Solace like the touch of angels,
Gave me joy and true rebirth,
Set me free and lost in wonder,
Blessed now of all the earth.

Acid

They ask for lyrical, I say why,
The train of thought not always sweet,
I write of life with warts and all,
Not always ordered never neat.

Pursuing dreams inside my head,
Pursuing consciousness or calm,
The words I write are of my time,
Not bent for healing or for harm.

The witches wove with spell and curse,
The prelates prattled down the years,
The words I write are of my time,
And shadow all my hopes and fears.

When I was young I walked with men,
That war had shattered or had made,
The cradling hand that gripped the gun,
The burning torch, the burnished blade.

And then the shadow of the bomb,
A shadow for the cloudless day,
We waited the apocalypse,
And danced the perfect nights away,

The revolutions never came,
The brave new world was not to be,
The protest songs were sung in-vain,
We never set the captives free.

Instead we fouled a wondrous world,
Our affluence has brought it low,
While rivers die we fill our cars,
To be where no one wants to go.

We weaken slowly with the years,
Both race and nation kith and kin,
We educate for what and why,
And make a virtue of our sin.

A link within an endless chain,
A glorious pattern, god's design,
If god sees man and owns his soul,
Why let his progress be malign.

The rain is falling on the blessed,
An acid rain to cleanse the earth,
What will we have when this is done,
The ghost of laughter, heavens mirth?

On a Visit to An Addiction Ward.

They told me she was damaged goods,
Broken like a china plate,
Face to the wall in an empty world,
No one to love no wit to hate.

Sometime someone's wonder child,
Dearly loved bright button new,
But now with rage and passion spent,
A darkened flame the tempest blew.

I look, I wonder and I see,
The selfishness that lies within,
Then place myself above it all,
And call the failing worse than sin.

Yet I am part as all are part,
My actions are not free from blame,
Call not on gods who may not hear,
We loosed this devil in their name.

Though she has sought a different way,
To find her soul and feel no pain,
The truth she tells has hurt my mind,
I will not visit here again.

Angelorum

Where are you now bright Urial,
When all the world is watching wise,
When love is bought, salvation sold,
And we are what the gods despise.

Brave Michael bold in helm and plate,
Once sure and mighty now a shade,
Who was with what and where and when,
And he who watched when all was made.

Of Raphael the tongues gave voice,
With words of rapture song and rhyme,
Who stands forgotten and alone,
A fable from another time.

Winged Gabriel the messenger,
For maid and shepherd and for me,
But still his message is not heard,
By those who never can be free.

And think of Lucifer the proud,
Cast down but never heavens slave,
Who wants and needs the second fall,
That leads we sinners to the grave,

Then calling home sweet gentle death,
In whose embrace is quiet rest,
Where silenced angels speak of peace,
And all is better than the best.

What shadows from the pages fly,
From scripture and the mystics word,
The seraphs tell and I must learn,
Yet live as though I never heard.

Child

There will be a child of man,
To wound the spirit, free the mind,
The gentle foe who sword in hand,
Lies cradled with the lowing kind.

There will be a child of man,
First born of woman, raised to pain,
Whose tears can turn a world to dust,
Or set the captive free again.

There will be a child of man,
Whose wrath will smite the mighty down,
Then god will smile when we are past,
And jewels flame the thorny crown.

There will be a child of man,
Whose blood is shed to empty sin,
When sacramental prayer is lost,
On he who saw the stars begin.

There will be a child of man,
Who dies upon the perfect day,
When food was all his every need,
And help was half a world away.

There will be a child of man,
A child of ours, a son of peace
Who easy on the emptied soul,
Will shower grace and bring release.

Christmas

So a child was born in Bethlehem,
But why should that matter to me,
When the children of Cain are legion,
In a world that may never be free.

Should I offer my tinsel and turkey,
As the songs of the season begin,
Or would a fast in the face of feasting,
Just mirror a deadlier sin.

Will I fear like Herod the mighty,
When I look to the stars up above,
Or climb once again to the hilltop,
And be lost in the sweet breath of love.

God grant me a new understanding,
To accept my position on earth,
And to know that there can be redemption,
In the treasures that come from rebirth.

For now that my years are ending,
May I first not forget but forgive,
And find in that great consolation,
A blessing and reason to live.

Conclusions

A Light That Shines In Darkness,
A Light That Darkness Cannot Overpower
                St John 1.

    Blind eyes on an iron angel,
    Blind faith in the pilgrim's way,
    This world of wonders waiting,
    For the endless ageless day.

    From the very edge of darkness,
    We have reached to heavens door,
    Have found and offered riches,
    And mastered even more.

    A potter's field for silver,
    A trade in heart and mind,
    The cruel and uncaring,
    The gentle and the kind.

    The mind of Torquemada,
    The art of Raphael,
    The searing truth in Francis,
    The Borgias gate to hell.

    A lighted hut in Auschwitz,
    The faith in a nation state,
    For as the gate is swinging,
    We are both love and hate.

We walk where none has trodden,
We watch the planet turn,
Where vanity is virtue,
And mighty cities burn.

But years are all as nothing,
A speck in a greater scheme,
So look for the love around you,
And look to the stars and dream.

When we conquer death and anger,
Will we suffer the blind to see,
Give life to this world of wonders,
And set her children free.

Will we be as a beacon in darkness,
A safe haven deep in the night,
And show to the whole of creation,
The glory and hope of the light.

Eyes on a Winter Page

Your eyes are on my winter page,
Each word like breath and fallen flowers,
While I have rhymes for many needs,
And treasures for the passing hours.

And did you read Gerontius,
Where Newman spoke of raging dreams,
Where hands offend to common prayer,
And Cranmer penned the precious reams.

I ponder and I quicken wit,
For words like masons stones can rise,
To truth and concert or to god,
Our worlds dissolved to bitter lies.

My Song of Solomon for fools,
My cause corrupt and cautions jape,
For those who seek but never find,
A food for swine, a wanton rape.

This father of a worthless child,
A mewling thing of fret and tears,
Who cast in syllable and line,
Was born of hope and fleeting years.

I strut a peacocks polished pride,
The wine of life an open cask,
I push the boundary, shade the lamp,
And daily wear a different mask.

Your eyes are on my winter page,
What value or what wisdom there,
What light illuminating gloom,
What sweet support to banish care.

I wade in meanings and I drown,
I climb ambition just to fall,
As vanity destroys my soul,
I hear damnations bugle call.

But in the rocks I anchor firm,
For life is just to those who try,
Full wise the wisdom of my age,
Full wise the man who knows the lie.

I anchor deep and anchor strong,
I triumph still no banners furled,
With pen and book as castle walls,
I set my verse against the world.

Forward

Cradle me now for I am a child,
The product of strength and of love,
The seed of humanity weak and yet wild,
A hawk to be fed by the dove.

Strengthen me now as I stand in my youth,
As I rage against all of your reason,
See in my eyes there's a different truth,
And mine are the years and the season,

Fear me now I am strong in my prime,
And the world is at last in my grip,
Sure of my age I can dominate time,
And nothing I order can slip.

Honour me now for you see I am old,
And the lingering days are so long,
And where is the hope when you're lonely and cold,
And where is the wine and the song.

So read from me now for I am your book,
And my pages record every trace,
Where each word is written if only you look,
In the mirror reflecting your face.

House

Hold fast the house against the wolf,
And from the howling in the night,
A breastplate for the scattered kin,
A radiance in the fading light.

A bridge that spans the flow of time,
A raft upon a splintered sea,
A heritage that all may claim,
A citadel that sets men free.

A house foursquare and founded deep,
No wave may crush or quake cast down,
For passion holds and love is strong,
While thorns still form a blessed crown.

With all our wit and all our dreams,
We forge and fret from year to year,
A potter's field for silver pence,
From Herod's rage and Pilot's fear.

The piercing lance the blooded cross,
And from this bleeding holy pain,
The house must stand or all is loss,
The sinless crucified again.

In The Eye of The Storm

Consider the ways of the whistling wind,
That turned the shaft in the millers tower,
That filled the sails and spun the stones,
And wrought the harvest into flour.

That bowed the masts of the clipper ships,
Who raced and chased against the sea,
From China to the Albion shore,
Full loaded with the precious tea.

So call upon the home of gales,
And whistle down the raging storm,
The ice bound blast to chill the bones,
The zephyrs kiss to make you warm.

And in the wind the breath of souls,
With mans first gasp when all was new,
An exhalation of the life,
The strongest wind that ever blew.

We take a breath and in the air,
We draw the breath from Adams lung,
And coursing through the open mouth,
Eternal songs the world has sung.

This wind to which we all give breath,
Has formed the words and made the lies,
And prelates, popes and heretics,
Have rattled out their silent cries.

We inhale Plato, breath out Proust,
And suck the air from Zion's hill,
We draw in tyrants, force out saints,
And thus the wind is never still.

So curse not bluster nor the cry,
This wind is perfect in us all,
The typhoon rages in the heart,
This storm was born before the fall.

Consider the ways of the whistling wind,
For it blows into your soul today,
The raging storm of endless years,
The gale that carries men away.

In The Shadow of Wings

No longer held no longer bound,
No longer fettered by the chains,
A grace released upon the wind,
When naught but sea and sky remains.

Where chains are forged by earthbound souls,
Though free from malice hard like stone,
The cording knot shall steal the breath,
And none but angels may atone.

So in the closing of my eyes,
Pass me then into life and birth,
From towering cliff to seek my way,
To own my wit and own my worth.

To soar above a cluttered world,
To test the storm and know the wave,
To look to what I never was,
A white winged shadow on my grave.

Some life to have when I am gone,
Whatever spirit follows through,
To wander like an ageless gull,
A blazing path to what is true.

For what are we, what do we know,
When chains confine the day and hour,
The bankers watch our every move,
And mice-like men have little power.

So give me wings and set me free,
To fly the confines of this jail,
As hope confounds we mount the cross,
And life drives in another nail.

So own the whirlwind bless the rain,
Take flight upon the wings of storm,
Embrace each raging icy blast,
And honour life in every form.

It may not come, I may not know,
For none of all return to tell,
But heaven needs the flight of souls,
To crush the vanities of hell.

Inheritance

Can we live in a world full of prophets,
Where the soothsayers smooth us with lies,
When lovers regale us with treasure,
Or beguile us with come to bed eyes.
When the dictionary empties its meanings,
To the voices we hear in our head,
And the fire is the pit of extinction,
When the wise and the worthy are dead.

Can we fly on the wings of an angel,
As the mountains are washed to the sea,
When our souls are as sand in a desert,
To be damned by the guilt in our plea.
When the child in our children is silenced,
By the burdens we load down the years,
Do we offer them sanctification,
Or the valley of terror and tears.

Can we walk with the saints and the sacred,
Being blinded to hatred and fear,
With the word as a helmet and breastplate,
And the hope of eternity near,
Or cross with the knowledge of nothing,
Being certain that nothing is there,
Being portion and part of oblivion,
Without rhyme or reason to care.

Labyrinth

I meet them in the labyrinth,
The lays of the dreaming soul,
They come to me with the folds of time,
To make me sound and whole.

Like knights in an ancient saga,
Or worms in the new turned earth,
They bless with the tongues of angels,
Or speak of the devils mirth.

Still I welcome the most and the many,
Like the comfort of clothes warm and worn,
And I grasp at the shades and the shadows,
Like the saint and the sinner reborn.

My parents are here and my lovers,
Good friends and the worst of my foe,
And the laughter rings out of my childhood,
In the place where my deep rivers flow.

And I touch them and tell in my dreaming,
All in blessing this happier time,
And I tell of no care for tomorrow,
As the sanctified touch the sublime.

But where is your song in this searching,
Will I raise you with equal acclaim,
Do I write for my own benediction,
And will you remember my name?

I have trusted and taken the bounty,
I have fallen and taken the pain,
I have loved both too well and too wisely,
And counted the loss as my gain.

But I still close my eyes in contentment,
For these visitors mean me no harm,
For the faces of friends and familiars,
Are as safe as my guardians arm.

For I feel that about and around me,
Is a precious and glorious light,
Not found for another mans darkness,
Not shown for another mans sight.

For the labyrinth holds all my reason,
Like a stone that is riven by gold
And while fire in my life is still burning
I must wait for the lays to unfold.

Lanes

There are times I wake distracted,
Distracted and bemused,
And times I wake with anger,
Both angry and confused

But life has taught me lessons,
That grief and pain are just,
When set against the tapestry,
Of lovers lies and burning lust.

You walk with your companions,
On lanes both long and wide,
But when you reach the forest,
You seek a place to hide.

For love can be confusion,
With ways to burn the soul,
But lost for good companions,
We never can be whole.

If dreams are made of wanting,
Then passions must be too,
For what are hopes but envy,
When dreams cannot come true.

For I have walked on empty lanes,
Both lonely and alone,
And cast my very dreams apart,
And set my heart to stone.

But still I learned my lesson,
For the lane was not too long,
To walk not yet a single mile,
And hear the sirens song.

When fire has melted even stone,
And lava drips like rain,
It's then the force of nature's hand,
Can steal away the pain.

When anger turns to solace sweet,
Distractions to the good,
Then I am Noah safe and saved,
And riding out the flood.

To set my footfall sound and dry,
My Ararat and castle keep,
The ark of safety close behind,
To save me from the raging deep.

Then lesson done I find my rest,
This lane has felt my homeward tread,
To wake at last content and safe,
With nothing more in life to dread.

Lateat Scintillula Forsan !

(The spark concealed)

When we call down the fire from heaven,
And are seared by the heat of the flame,
What we kindle so soon will be ashes,
Where no man remembers our name.

Like a tree standing high on the hillside,
Rooted firm on the primeval stone,
We are shocked by the thunderbolts quiver,
Crying helpless and lost and alone.

We can dream with the dreams of the ancients,
Casting runes for the gods in our head,
Where the faith of the many is fruitless,
And hopes of the people are dead.

Yet the spark from above is salvation,
Like the staff that is comfort and calm,
Where the ampulla waits with the kingdom,
And the sceptre and sword bear no harm.

When the spear and the nails lead to glory,
Where a scaffold is passion and pride,
Where love is a promise eternal,
And only destruction has died.

I may reach but my heart will not find it,
Being more than confusion can hold,
But I look with the eyes of conviction.
At a treasure more precious than gold.

I would call down the fire from the heavens,
And be seared by the heat of the flame,
For soon I will be as the ashes,
And none will remember my name.

License to What

I'm minded to a Christmas where the happy tills don't ring,
Where plastic reindeer never go and santa's elves don't sing,
I'm minded to a Christmas where the gaudy lights are gone,
And high above a waiting world a single star has shone.

There's something in simplicity that stirs the very soul,
That makes an atheist like me at least a little whole,
For past and childhood press on me like comforts cleansing sigh,
And leave me with a longing that I'm too quick to deny.

The gothic church that cradled me was sombre dark and cold,
Not half as old as Christendom with half its tales untold,
The light through leaded windows was a riotous coloured blaze,
Of saints and martyrs sanctified to chasten and amaze.

But in the cold December days the transept was transformed,
And I transported and transfixed with all my senses stormed,
Would watch with eyes of wonder as the Christ child entered in,
Emanuel 'god with us' and a saviour slaying sin.

But there's nothing of that wonder in the things I see today,
A secular St Nicholas with parcels on a sleigh,
A Bernard Mathews turkey with some stuffing on the side,
A larger glass of whisky and a sumptuous dose of pride.

A feast of office parties where we flirt and preen and strut,
Like many rabid rabbits or the roe-deer in the rut,
With fibre optic tinselled trees that make a gentle glow,
God rest we merry gentlemen so little do we know.

That's why I'm off to different lands and on some foreign shore,
I'll spend a quiet Christmas time with she who I adore,
And maybe half a world away in some quite heathen land,
I'll find the truth of Christian peace and maybe understand.

For surely we have lost it in this vast commercial mill,
It's grinding us inexorably; we're bending to its will,
And deep in all my longings is the need to get it back,
And set my wayward train of life upon some different track.

I hope that in the deserts waste a distant star will shine,
A tiny glow within my heart entire, entirely mine,
A carol for the innocent that once was only me,
The song of songs enrapturing that sets a sinner free.

Thus may we find this Christmastide a blessing on us all?
Be we the lauded mighty or the subjugated small,
Be we the wretched prisoner or the keeper of the cell,
Who offer now of friendships hand and close the gates of hell.

For somewhere in a silent street in long millenniums past,
A hope to fill a million dreams yet give one dream to last,
A touchstone for a better life that shines as diamond bright,
And leaves a dark and shattered world the gospel of the light.

Marrakech Expressions

The road that runs south from the Atlas,
Came thundering into the day,
As we were bound for Marrakech,
Two hundred miles away.

The wild desert sands were all singing,
Sounding songs from a time that is past,
Where the devil gets lost in the detail,
As the nets of the mystics are cast.

For the old city seethed with her children,
Sending smoke scented sound to the air,
A pearl set with silks and with spices,
Though a she wolf at bay in her lair.

The sun was as warm as her welcome,
But the wind from the mountain blew cold,
While the valley unfolded her secrets,
She whispered of tales never told.

Of the age of the wandering nomad,
Of the spice road that ran to the west,
Of the slaves that were sold where we pondered,
Of the traders who came here to rest.

Yet we saw in the sprawl and the squalor,
A glimmer of things we have lost,
To a timelessness found without freedom,
We surrendered without count for cost.

We left feeling slightly uneasy,
Like the burden of partial regret,
As the moon set to silver the desert,
Matching gold where a soft sun had set.

We know we will never go back there,
But romance will recapture the glow,
Of a city of dreams in the desert,
Where only true dreamers should go.

Monster

Shimmering gold on November trees,
And hardened words in harder print,
Unwanted, hounded to the grave,
With curses shouted sharp as flint.

And so to this my living creed,
I seek no god, I will not bow,
I cleave firm to humanity,
And dwell within the here and now.

And so without a deity,
I find a code by which to live,
A hopeful place without a god,
Where love has taught me to forgive.

For at the last when hope is gone,
The chalice falls outside our grip,
We ask forgiveness and from what,
The shadows come, the powers slip,

The mirror shines reflective, bright,
The mighty flame within us lit,
But if with pride we dim the light,
We fall corrupted to the pit.

Forgive again and live the word,
Count not the times, count not the crime,
For grace and love I cry forgive,
And place not enmity in time.

I ask forgiveness here and now,
From those I challenge or offend,
For love is my beatitude,
To all who call mankind a friend.

May peace at last be all our hope,
When consolation empties fears,
The monsters dust is in the earth,
One tear among a million tears.

On The Death Of A Notorious Mass Murderer

Oblivion

Seek me out not as a stranger,
Comfort me not as a foe,
Hold me when others reject me,
Travel the roads I must go.

Know me when I am confusion,
Feel for the end of my day,
Study my route to oblivion,
Take all the troubles away,

Deep in the mist of seclusion,
Whisper of things that are past,
Shatter the night with delusion,
Count not the dice that are cast.

Live liberty as a passion.
Trust life as the essence of me,
For chained once again by my freedom,
True loving is setting me free.

Outlook

We watch in the night as the stars look down,
And we see only lights in the blue-black sky,
No vestige of heaven surmounting the cloud,
No hope in the distance refuting the lie.

As creatures of spirit we search in the book,
For as Ahab the king we are cursed in our birth,
Regarded by men as the house on the rock,
We are founded by angels an object of mirth.

There are tales in the scriptures to burden the soul,
And joys in corruption to saver and save,
In Solomon's song is a refuge for men,
And a hope for redemption this side of the grave.

We have burdened the blind and have pleasured the rich,
Offered debt to the destitute, toil to the weak,
Ploughed up the fields when the seed corn was sown,
Empowering Caesar when mercy would speak.

We have loved and have hated have bartered and sold,
Like the thief in the temple that tore at the veil,
We have wounded salvation with hammer and spear,
But have not found the reason to reach for the grail.

We will watch in the night while the stars still look down,
And will watch for the coming as mans ages fly,
Then raised up anointed both blessing and blessed,
We will shout the great whisper and trumpet the sigh.

Pax Americanus.

The Jackals cry to a desert moon,
On haunted mourning shivered sands,
Like lovers lost on long dead seas,
Or ancient gods in ancient lands.

For while the watchers wait and stare,
We gaze behind the stellar wall,
Armed like none were ever blessed,
To rise and rape the bugle call.

What sylphlike beauty fills the sky,
And with what stealth the lover comes,
With sweet caress the fire and flame,
With symphony the pipe and drums.

I feel my hand is on the sword,
The scimitar beneath my heel,
My challenger like Abrahams,
Has broken wide the seventh seal.

My blood is spilling on the ground,
It cries to heaven, heaven blessed,
For I am righteous with the worst,
And offer passions with the best.

Crusader knight with cross held high,
Too proud a boast, too grand the aim,
We come to save or so we say,
God's blessing by another name.

And will they write of living saints,
And enemies recount us well,
Will heaven smile as women weep,
While children count the tolling bell.

I see the wall, the list of names,
The heroes showered with poppies red,
We sing to laud the fallen few,
And sanctify the nameless dead.

Rainscape

It is a summer Sunday and the rain from heaven pours,
Despite the spirits willingness I'm here confined indoors,
The riot that is summers growth is blessing bush and tree,
And I am feeling miserable and being little me.

On days like this with time to think I view the broader sphere,
And can't accept the truth of what the pundits make me hear,
The sporting life is seen by some like hope the holy grail,
While strikes against the sainted few will make the nation fail.

We hold our own opinions we'll not perceive a need,
Not always due to carelessness and rarely due to greed
We often think the third time what is right or best ignored,
And what is for the common good or better off deplored.

Disease they say in Africa will blight ten million lives,
And war that stalks the bible lands makes widows of the wives,
The situations round the world just tend to leave us cold,
When lives are made and mangled by the mouthy and the bold.

I'm probably a bigot or perhaps just something worse,
I couldn't face a conscience or an inner need to nurse,
I harbour right wing tendencies that build with passing years,
And nurture xenophobia to best allay my fears.

Will god 'if he can influence us' look down and give us health,
The state provides and will protect while taxing all our wealth,
The prelates chant theocracy while simple men bow low,
And in the end for all mankind there's just one place to go.

And thus it is, and thus it was, and thus it all shall be,
The rain beyond the windowpane has nourished every tree,
The church roof in the distance bears the lichen and the moss,
And we are living in a world that doesn't care a toss.

For lichen grips like poverty and moss it grows like pain,
And still some beg contentment from the need that comes again,
We pour out from our substance to the things we think are right,
And satisfy the demons when they prod us in the night.

A blessing on the men of peace and blessings on the poor,
These great and graced beatitudes lay broken on the floor,
What comfort to the world remains when faced with joyous sin,
Who marks our doors for Passover, when death comes stealing in.

And yet and yet and yet and yet an endless ageless cry,
Tomorrow may be better and give history the lie,
Apocalyptic horsemen ride and rain from clouds of dream,
And musings on a rainy day are never what they seem.

Remittance

I'll tell you gently if I can,
About the last remittance man,
Whose epithets were lies and lust,
Whose honesty you could not trust,
Who yet inside his failing fault,
Could give your sober sense a jolt.

A man of wit and sometimes jest,
A little better than the rest,
Of agile mind and stunning tale,
Whose confidence could never fail,
Who vainly faulted was from birth,
A scourge upon this blessed earth.

He sowed his seed in many fields,
And never counted up the yields,
The daughters and the feckless spouse,
Were welcomed to his bawdy house,
And comfort given bold delight,
He pleasured most of every night.

The drink! I wish I could explain,
Perhaps it took away the pain,
From he who spoke in stunted verse,
Of all his passions pride and worse,
But wine will have the truth they say,
To cast the demons far away.

But I have loved him, God knows why,
Through every crime and every lie,
For blood will out as days may run,
Till time on earth is lost or done,
For gods are dreams that poets write,
While wit and realm and rhyme take flight.

So if his bones are dust and more,
Upon some blighted foreign shore,
Then I will weep and wring my hands,
And curse that grave in foreign lands,
Yet cry rejoice and bless him free,
Whose joys and vanities are me.

Rolling Back The Stone

As a child I was washed by the stories,
A theology heavy as stone,
A mystery locked in a black bounded book,
And as brittle as sanctified bone.

Yet willing I walked to the darkness,
And snuffed out the innermost light,
For the darkness had offered me shelter,
And conquered the fear of the night.

There Lazarus stood at my elbow,
As I languished with him in the tomb,
And the light that would be resurrection,
Was shut from my windowless room.

So I ploughed in the deserts of strangers,
Though I held fertile lands of my own,
And gleaned the last ears from the stubble,
While striding the darkness alone.

But for each soul there waits a redeemer,
Be it time or the ancient of days,
For who knows the face of his saviour,
And who dares pronounce on his ways.

As I gathered my bounty around me,
I found it was clinker and ash,
And the things that I valued were worthless,
For my treasures were tawdry and trash.

So I raged in my sepulchre prison,
As you rage at the inflowing sea,
And I cursed at my own misconception,
Of what could be perfect or free.

Then I clawed at the walls with my fingers,
Till my nails were both bloody and raw,
But the rock that I'd placed in the doorway,
I knew could be moved nevermore.

But outside my whole comprehension,
Was tomorrow disguised as today,
A light born to shatter the darkness,
By a creature of comfort and clay.

The tomb it had rotted my senses,
But my visions detected the light,
As the stone was rolled back from the doorway,
My mind was enraptured and bright.

There were gods in the air on that evening,
There was light on elysian fields,
And I was a soul set for heaven,
And content for whatever life yields.

So seek for the inner contentment,
Preparing to roll back the stone,
Or walk to the shadow of darkness,
And be lost and forever alone.

Shades and Shadows

When the shades of my past come singing,
In the light of a waxing moon,
Then who would I be to deny them,
Or offer a different tune.

When God is an imperfect stranger,
And life is an endless plain,
Then where would I see my horizon,
Or seek out my highway again.

For the shadows of those who have taught me,
Are marking each verse and each rhyme,
And I cannot yet ask their forgiveness,
For they have yet no place in my time.

To the ghosts of the many who loved me,
Who live only when I speak their name,
Will you tell in heaven above me,
That no man is free of his shame.

Hold fast to the good in your spirit,
Acknowledge the right and the wrong,
Be true to your past, to the die that is cast,
And wait for sweet memories song.

Singing to The Silence

There will be a time for the silence,
To be heard again after the call,
To be heard with the final trumpet,
To be sanctified after the fall.

When the gates of the chantry are opened,
As the souls of the faithful gain grace,
What then will be left but the silence,
Or what should be left in its place.

When the tolling of bells ends the quiet,
And the keening of saints rends the air,
Pale horses will carry their riders,
To open the seals of despair.

And what will be left for the morning,
When our rages are over and done,
Will the world still awaken to birdsong,
Will the flowers still turn to the sun.

Will the timeless waves beat on the seashore,
Will the lightning still shatter the trees,
Will the soft sands still swirl in the desert,
Will the flowers still dance in the breeze.

Will the lion still stalk the savannah,
Will the eagle still circle the skies,
Will the stars still caress from the heavens,
Will the new truth prove histories lies.

For we fete both the wanton and wicked,
While despising the wise and the meek,
As the prophet plays harlequin angel,
Singing hymns for the old and the weak.

When I dance with my life in abandon,
As the runes tell of things that are past,
The church door lies broke on its hinges,
And the dice of corruption are cast.

For the clock in the tower is ticking,
Like a heartbeat it's sounding the knell,
And as god calls the world to salvation,
The beast calls the faithless to hell.

Stand guard in the hall of the ancients,
And take swords to the rope and the knot,
Offer only the wisdom of children,
To the world that the seraphs forgot,

For the silence must yield to the singing,
As the beast yields to light from above,
When we sing with the music unwritten,
We will sing to the silence of love.

Spider

The spider that clung to the stable wall,
Knew nothing of the day,
All she knew was the tail of the ox,
Had carried her web away.

The spider on the manger rail,
Knew nothing of what was said,
All she saw was a crying child,
As she fastened another thread.

The spider ringed by her silken trap,
Knew nothing of shepherds there,
All she heard was the angel's song,
As she clung to the gossamer stair,

The spider still in her shimmering orb,
Knew nothing of three wise men,
All that she sensed was the scent of myrrh,
As she crept to her silent den.

The spider that spun in the crook of the cross
Knew nothing of the day,
All she knew was the clamouring men,
Had carried her web away.

Sunflowers

We think to grow our sunflowers,
With dreams we set the seeds,
Embrace and nurture what we sow,
A garden in the weeds.

We feed them with the wit of man,
Protect them from the cold,
And make them hardy for the time,
When flowers must be sold.

When pestilence would cut them down,
We rush to make them strong,
And make for them the sheltering,
Against wild winters song.

A bud at first so tight and green,
A fist that grasps a stone,
Like greyhounds standing in the slips,
The strong must stand alone.

And then they bloom like comforts cause,
A dream that fills the eyes,
The inmost light, the brightest star,
The love that never dies.

Or so it's said or so it seems,
Beguiling us with wonder,
But thoughts to nothing often fade,
And break the world asunder.

For sunflowers are like fleeting thought,
Like dreams that fade and die,
The strength of spring in yesterday,
The clouding mist, the lover's lie.

But soon will come the fallow time,
When bare earth cries for seed,
A time to plant for multitudes,
Where intellect will lead.

A time to think of spring again,
Where sunflowers seek the light,
Where mindful men can turn the world,
Full precious in the right.

When gods reflect on mans desire,
When fear will drift away,
And I will be a sunflower then,
The blossom for the day.

Swimmers

I watch the swimmers in the air,
The birds, the bats and butterflies,
With rivers in the flowing winds,
And oceans in the endless skies.

All this creation startles wit,
Confuses reason, storms the mind,
They rise on seas intangible,
And leave a tawdry world behind.

And in such flight we see our dreams,
Like mirrored lanterns in the night,
The hopes that rise like wafted down,
All sanctified and feathered light.

But like the swimmers we are caught,
By ebb and current time and tide,
And flowing thoughtless through the years,
We conjure love and harvest pride.

And by the time we know our minds,
The trap is sprung and we are caught,
We seek the caves of solitude,
But cannot hide from inner thought.

They say to cause the gods to laugh,
First tell them boldly of your plan,
Oh little hope, Oh faulted dream,
Oh mighty fate, Oh little man.

For still above us all they soar
Like plague, contagious, touching all,
Our dreams when made and manifest,
Are of mankind before the fall.

For what are we but ghosts or gods,
Or even swimmers in our time,
We live the moment and the day,
We revel in our pride and prime.

So watch the swimmers in the air,
They too must find a place to rest,
The eagle at the mountain top,
The wasp within the paper nest.

I showed the gods my perfect plan,
And I amused them with my fears,
They toyed with me and set me down,
And shadowed me through all my years.

So still I battle with the gale,
The breath of god that steals my heart,
When earthly bonds are perfect pain,
And nothing rends my hope apart.

I swim in passion warm and deep,
I drown in oceans set with dreams,
The plan that god could not endure,
Is all and everything it seems.

Teddy Bear

At first I only saw the flowers,
Like rich brocade a wayside altar,
The bright of nature, sweet in air,
That caused my onward step to falter.

But then my gaze fell to the toys,
The string and tape that held them there,
Festooning all to a crash scarred tree.
And crying out for the world to care.

I did not stop to read the notes,
That cruel rain had blurred to scrawl,
But walking on reviewed the scene,
And wondered do we care at all.

The tree still unforgiving stands,
And will another hundred years,
While wife or mother waits and weeps,
And wraps herself in happened fears.

With quickening step I cross the road,
But can't resist the backward glance,
The wind has skirled the marigolds,
And set the teddy bear to dance.

A masque macabre, a cabaret,
A puppet master to the spheres,
The bear performs its pirouette,
While no one looks and no one hears.

And strangely I am forced to smile,
As blood is quickened through each vein,
I hear from deep inside my soul,
A keening song that brings me pain.

The tree is scarred and I am too,
Diminished, damaged, and amazed,
But yet without the mortal shock,
I feel the man within me raised.

These shrines adorn our city streets,
But flowers fade, corrupt and die,
And all will be as it has been,
When memories are just a lie.

For we are only fading blooms,
And toys that dance to the wind of change,
Tied to our tree by a greater hand,
And plans the fates can't re-arrange.

Tempus Fugit

Ten thousand sapphires in the night,
The perfect peerless diadem,
In endless age and ageless end,
This myriad this faultless gem.

These stars that shine enlisting years,
Before the years were first begun,
When time in stream began to flow,
With all as new and nothing done.

Mans time these heavens cast aside,
His concept vanity with age,
The deeper stream runs on and on,
More fathomless than wit may gauge.

And yet we pray to bless our lives,
God grant us what or this or why,
We count the days the fleeting hours,
And edge to death with every lie.

For time we count is time we made,
The moments are of mans design,
We count each sunset mark each day
By breaking bread and drinking wine.

For if god counts as we presume,
What mysteries are in his ken,
The ageless endless winds the clock,
And binds with chain the hopes of men.

The gate is open mark the way,
The paths lead on with no way back,
The light is always in our eyes,
The past like nowhere cold and black.

While angels guard the doors of death,
These portals stand with fettered gate,
We enter periled bound in fear,
The graceless in the graceless state.

So light the beacon feed the flame,
For time will soon extinguish all,
And we will be as angels then,
Like Adam was before the fall.

Then turn the page and bless the day,
Sweet time like us will soon be gone,
When god is first and last and all,
The first the last and only one.

The Church of the Nativity

This is not a quiet place,
The crowds surround yet all is calm,
Where years and nations fade away,
And is no fear and no alarm.

For here within what son of man,
Could fail to sense the weight of time,
Bright brazen star, smoke blackened stone,
An anvil for a reasoned rhyme.

I feel the pebble in my shoe,
A pilgrims stone to cause me pain,
No rapture here, an emptying,
To know I'll not return again.

This place that contrasts god and man,
What bitter sweetness fills my mind,
All justice here and all regret,
Ambition falters, love is blind.

I leave and I will not look back,
I cast my pebble to the ground,
There still are shepherds on the hills,
And still my saviour to be found.

The Interpretation of Dreams

We have a need to sit and dream,
We have a need to wonder,
When all our aims are cast aside,
And hopes are set asunder.

We live like deer or shy gazelle,
Our resting place the sun filled glade,
But waiting at the forest edge,
The yellowed fang the sharpened blade.

But dream we will as dream we must,
Imaginations feed our mind,
And be they passions lust or love,
They teach our souls to loose and bind.

If we ourselves could mirror god,
What true reflections would we see,
The breath of angels in the heart,
Soft earth to plant the knowledge tree,

If we accept that we are dust,
Why crawl primeval from the slime,
We burnish hope like glistered gold,
With dreams to light the lamp of time.

When we aspire the mountains shake,
For naught but dread can hold us down,
We turn the tides on endless shores,
And cause the fearing hordes to drown.

Our greatest art has capture light,
The music soars in unchained spheres,
We bless the page with written word,
Our songs have echoed down the years.

And all in all we sit and dream,
The physicist the engineer,
The poet and the courtesan,
The prisoner, the pioneer.

And yet within our sun filled glade,
The frail gazelle that is our mind,
Must quiet stand and wait the shock,
That comes to deafen and to blind.

For in our dreams the tigers wait,
With yellowed teeth and glinting eye,
When all of hope is hopelessness,
And life has been a bitter lie.

The Knowing of Time

I will know that I've reached my time,
When the summers are endless and still,
When the songbirds are with me in chorus,
While the pleasures still lift me and thrill.

When the mountains are crested with glory,
As I hold the whole world in my hands,
And I lust with the touch of a lover,
In a passion my muse understands,

With my footfall on long golden highways,
And my eyes set where wisdom has reign,
I can shout in that moment of triumph,
That the gods have released me from pain.

But I know well with all that is in me,
And with all that is told from the past,
That the years of a man are not endless,
And that pleasures and passions not last.

There is coming a time for forgiveness,
Where the child in the man will succeed,
When love will be all that flows onward,
From the rivers of envy and greed.

For when pride in my conquest has faded,
When I've written my absolute rhyme,
Then by my hand or that of another,
I will know that I'm reaching my time.

The Lost

Cold in the wind wild dawn of dream I rise,
Life in each moment bold around my ear,
I take to my living the evil I despise,
And hold to each and each the movement that I fear.

Night in the cold black peace of passing day,
Steals like the wind into my lonely mind,
I cast my eyes onto my weary feet of clay,
Seeking that which lost I know I cannot find.

The cold wet leaves of autumn pave my road,
Each golden death in glory stains my way,
Not one of all I meet will help me bear my load,
Or tell me what these mists of winter say.

The stars the million lanterns of the dawn,
Break on my solitude the portals of my sleep,
And backward look into my dreams and all forlorn,
Gaze into the endless day and weep.

My life once free is fettered to this place,
My soul a bird now bounded by this cage,
I hold my shuttered eyes and hide my face,
While heart and mind in desperation rage.

The only verses to survive my first marriage

The Substance of Angels

I have surely walked with angels,
Through my deepest darkest night,
Called to comfort they have held me,
Brought me safely to the light.
At my heels the prince of devils,
Demon herds like screaming swine,
All they promised was my glory,
Sweet contentment, heady wine.

See within this pale reflection,
Mirrored by the blackest flame,
He who fell but still is calling,
Calling me to own his name.
Touch a hand and feel the pleasure,
Drawn and damned to dreams sublime,
Flourish then in fallen nature,
Lost to hope and slaves to time.

Swords like lightning clashed above me,
Shields like scripture braced my soul,
Lambs blood daubed above the doorway,
Passing over, safe and whole.
I have surely walked with angels,
They like lovers claim my heart,
I can feel their arms enfold me,
Close and caring not apart.

Lead me on to greater wonders,
Knowing though that I must fail,
Bondsman to my pride and anger,
Peace to be my holy grail.
Heap and burn my earthly riches,
Melt my envy in the blaze,
Lead me to the aesthetes treasure,
Cast aside my wayward ways.

I can hear the seraphs footfall,
Lighter than the falling snow,
Pointed whispered words of comfort,
Telling me the way to go.
If god there is and god is listening,
Maybe this is just a prayer,
I have needed these companions,
Both in hope and dark despair.

Still I see the dark ones waiting,
Raging, lusting for my brain,
Comprehending all my reason,
Authors then of all my pain.
Make me then to walk with angels,
Armed by them against the storm,
Messengers of greater glory,
Spirits sent in earthly form.

To Emptiness

He drinks and I must excuse him,
The bottle more friendly than me,
While others revile and abuse him,
A soul without senses is free.

In a very real way he's my brother,
Though he's lost in a world of his own,
In a place without structure or reason,
Where only the memories atone.

I forgive with forgiveness a habit,
And I distance myself from his pain,
Then I laugh with the others around him,
And compound his failing again.

When I reach for a glass to make merry,
Its oblivion that glares in my eye,
For I cannot accept what is in me,
And this truth is the absolute lie.

So drink to his health as a stranger,
As he drinks to his death every day,
He has truly found hope in the spirit,
And a lover that never will stray.

Two

When I had childish innocence,
I spread my arms to hold the earth,
No rapture but my mothers smile,
When safe and sure was all my worth.

I saw a child some days ago,
Sleeping, cradled, comfort calm,
A lifesprings wonder slumber still,
In whom no trouble nor alarm.

Then to my mind crept bitter winds,
That spoke of days and years to come,
Of love and loss and emptiness,
Of pain that renders angels dumb.

These winds that are the lot of man,
Teach all our kind to fear the light
We children of the summers day,
Are slaves unto the darker night.

But in the quickened infant form,
Are hopes begot in adult fears,
We send our offspring to their fate,
And send our essence down the years.

The sum of all that ever were,
The sum of all that are to be,
Each child though neither kith nor kin,
Is part and all of you and me.

The candles flame through summer days,
The flowers shrivel where they lie,
We wake to solace in the dawn,
And pray for those who had to die.

We fall diminished, faulted, frail,
Like grains of sand upon the shore,
But rise exalted, royal rare,
Where evermore is evermore.

Writing

We took some pens to Africa don't ask the reason why,
You'd think we carried half the world to cloud a southern sky,
We didn't think and first world eyes were blinded by our pride,
And dust bowl roads were worlds away from home truths that have lied.

I half expected poverty, I half expected pain,
I half expected emptiness on some forgotten plain,
With half remembered memories of lessons as a child,
That told of tolling mission bells that sanctified the wild.

But what I found was different and still I am confused,
A land that I have visited and feel I have abused,
Not confident colonial hands had made a better life,
For those whose independent thought still fills the world with strife.

I'd tried to get a handle on the culture I would face,
So in my surly English way I'd fit into the place,
I'd got my head round Asia and Brazil was not a chore,
But for the price of conscience coin this place would cost me more.

I went to see the wildlife and the people were the rest,
The human kind were secondary and less than second best,
I saw their squalor, turned my head and focused far away,
These sights and sounds of Africa I didn't want to stay.

So elephants and wildebeest the evening lions roar,
And half a million wading birds on some bright blighted shore,
The luxury of lodges that well cater for the few,
And all the pleasures we deserve for being me and you.

And then it bites you and it drones like some mosquitoes flight,
For when you settle down to rest in comfort for the night,
A half a mile away or less a child of nine or ten,
Must live and bear a burden that would crush us lesser men.

I flew back home from Africa and really it was flight,
I couldn't settle all my thoughts and something wasn't right,
I knew I was discomforted but still can't find the word,
And in my soul the song I hear would better not be heard.

And so back to the pens we took to that far distant land,
Perhaps within the words to write is cause to understand,
Miracles are best prepared by scabbarding the sword,
And if the pen is mightier then that is due reward.

And so to some forgotten child in some forgotten place,
A child of the beatitude a child without a face,
Who takes a pen with childlike faith and someday in her prime,
Will write the words that alter worlds and change the face of time.

Zen

I hear the sound of one hand clapping,
Distant, dulcet and divine,
One hand graced by exaltation,
One hand reaching out for mine.

Love is like an endless circle,
Sweet circumference closed the ring,
Souls together one hand clapping,
Rich inside the echoing.

Raise the noise of one hand clapping,
Raise it till it stills the throng,
When you feel the roaring silence,
Feel your soul be raised to song.

When we take then we must empty,
When we give we fill again,
Peace triumphant one hand clapping,
Floods to mercy, empties pain.

Note and nurture what is given,
Enmity the great charade,
Listen then to one hand clapping,
Of this sound the world is made.

Gods of justice feel the motion,
When the wind blows hard and chill,
Cast and claimed by one hand clapping,
Never quieted, never still.

Rivers flow and seas accept them,
Men return to ash and dust,
Like the sense of one hand clapping,
We release both life and lust.

Place your trust in what is ageless,
Knowing what your heart demands,
Whispered words in one hand clapping,
Singing like the shifting sands.

Hear me now and mind my message,
Listen to the soundless spheres,
There is joy in one hand clapping,
If the seeker seeks and hears.

Lift me to the highest mountains,
Sink me in the deepest lakes,
Let me learn how one hand clapping,
All of lesser thought forsakes.

Sweet redemption be my calling,
Sweet forgiveness my reward,
Hear the sound of one hand clapping,
That which cast away the sword.

The Politics of Humour

A Tax on Both Your Houses

Have you noticed how election time brings out the very best,
How each and every party is much better than the rest,
From councillors to ministers they strut and preen and pout,
And do the very best they can to get each other out.

No policy is too extreme nor flight of fancy base,
No promise can be overlooked in this selective race,
Where cabinets are made of men and often women too,
Who shout to fortify the red and bolster up the blue.

The party politic they say is democratic balm,
We vote them in and vote them out and thus can do no harm,
But what I say for all of this is look back down the years,
And ponder just what they have done for laughter and for tears.

The careless cruel and clumsy, the feckless and benign,
The statesmen who were rounded by the women and the wine,
The radicals who in my youth regaled the baying hordes,
And found themselves in latter years as ermine coated lords.

I stand as an observer just a dreamer with a vote,
The kind of unsophisticate that keeps the ship afloat,
This ship of state has come to ground on many hidden rocks,
When turkeys vote for christmas and the chickens for the fox.

Self-seeking no it cannot be just altruistic zeal,
And yet within my deepest soul that isn't what I feel,
A politician wouldn't lie and scandalise my mind,
They truly strive and sacrifice to ease my daily grind.

I thank them for the Income Tax that really set me free,
Though even when I've paid it all there is nothing left for me,
I love the vehicle excise and the duty on my wine,
And fuel tax and V.A.T. have left me feeling fine.

Just look at local government another worthwhile band,
Our councillors are paragons a credit to the land,
Each one a servant of us all, have gratitude for that,
So smile each time your council tax comes thudding on the mat.

And when you die with any luck they'll grab another slice,
Your kids should not inherit as it wouldn't quite be nice,
And thus they tax my bank account to help me scrimp and save,
So I can help the chancellor when tucked up in my grave.

So death and taxes certainly are all we have to fear,
The politicians make the rules but never seem to hear,
So I misquote with good intent, without a hint of shame,
And in our nations breathless rush pay-up and play the game.

All Downhill From Here

The summer I was twenty was the time I saw things clear,
A motorbike and rock and roll and all downhill from here,
A girlfriend with the wilder streak whose scent was like the night,
And I was Ajax sword in hand to set the world to right.

We sang of revolution and we revelled in our youth,
For we had faith and fortitude and we had power and truth,
For we were British right or wrong our place was at the top,
No place for johnny foreigner, the cream of every crop.

The summer I was thirty I had mapped out my career,
The father of two children it was all downhill from here,
You can't expect a Rolls Royce but you've got the company car,
And the mortgage leaves you pennies you're collecting in a jar.

The mistresses you've hidden on the corporate account,
A booming brave economy that never makes you doubt,
A fugitive from real and true, a slave to business greed,
And always what you really want and never what you need.

The summer I was forty was the time to stand and jeer,
It seemed I'd almost made it and its all downhill from here,
I watched my school contemporaries all slide the greasy pole,
And combed the grey in shattered locks that once were black as coal.

The fees for education that the state could not provide,
Not really a necessity but some small cause for pride,
With interest rates at twelve percent, a balance in the red,
And many many sleepless nights in many a lonely bed.

The summer I was fifty I was made morose by fear,
Both heavier and weaker it was all downhill from here,
I learned that two old schoolmates were as worm-food in the grave,
And pain within the troubled heart bode nothing sure to save.

The salutary warnings and the serpents tooth of pain,
The gold ring of redemption and the passion without stain,
The chalice of beginnings and the wholesome bread of truth,
And light within the tunnel that is evidence and proof.

The summer I was sixty gave a different star to steer.
Thank god I see retirement and its all downhill from here,
The goals that once were precious were a gilded leaden chain,
And little of ambitions lust has fortune, price or pain.

For now I have the pleasure of the comfortable and dear,
And though it may be all down hill, and all down hill from here,
Though memory has gentle slopes and precipices steep,
It sets within the consciousness, a winding way to keep.

Automobelia

The cars I had bring memories,
They mark each month and year,
To aged fool from callow youth,
They mapped the road I steer.

I fed them with the very best,
To every need complied,
A very metal essence,
That could never be denied.

It was in the nineteen sixties,
That I bought my very first,
Be certain not the best car,
And probably the worst.

It cost me twenty eight pounds ten,
Inclusive of the tax,
But sure as sure when driving it,
You never could relax.

With cable brakes, no synchromesh,
To drive it needed skill,
It handled like a bloated whale,
Full guaranteed to thrill.

On hotter days the thing would boil,
And rain would see it stop,
It rolled demented down the hills,
And groaned the summits top.

Too often it would need a push,
Electrics flat and dead,
I'd have to leave it in the lane,
And bus it home instead.

I'd thought 'a magnet for the girls',
Dark glimmers in my mind,
But often they would bus it home,
And leave me there behind.

And still I loved it rust and all,
Its leather and its wood,
It never did me any harm,
Though doing little good.

It never got me into debt,
All through my student years,
It brought me lots of laughter,
And as oft frustrations tears.

From Reliant to the odd Rolls Royce,
By now I've owned the lot,
From Bubble Cars to Yankee flash,
I've caused their rise and rot.

They led me to the open road,
In ways they set me free,
But even as I drive in them,
In truth they're driving me.

December Musings

The Santa was fat and lugubrious, his beard was nylon spun,
He stood beside the grotto gate his duties nearly done,
The light had faded from the sky and dappled it into night,
And icy drops of chilling rain were putting the crowds to flight.

The credit cards had done their worst and the shelves were nearly bare,
The rich had loaded the four by fours and who was left to care,
The turkeys in the butchers shop were offered at bargain price,
And in the bars the sweet red wine was mulled with cloves and spice.

But a world away from the shopping mall the picture is less serene,
Though the bells will ring and the candles glow what will the season mean,
For I've stood in the place where the story began that we took for the start of our time,
And have looked for the ages and reason of man, and have looked for the cause sublime.

The prelates have told me and often I heard that I walk in the full sight of god,
The psalmist has written and once I believed in the comfort of his staff and rod,
To fail and to falter is nature to man, forgiveness the deities' boon,
Should we fall into darkness and burn in the pit or just seek for redemption too soon.

In the place of nativity sooty and dark, the flags were both broken and cracked,
A place for salvation, a place built for hope, or just for the faith that I lacked,
The pious and hopeful, the watchers like me, we stood in the incense filled air,
But the city of mammon an eon away was fixed in my mind distant stare.

So back to my Christmas, my cold Yorkshire Street, the Santa's lugubrious grin,
I know what I'm wanting I know what I'll give and I know that I'll yield to the sin,
And just as resisting the Bethlehem child is as easy as writing my name,
Mistaking the meaning of what I see now, do I have my misgivings to blame?

I'll send out the cards with Dickensian scenes and bless that more comforting day,
We'll go to the pantomime, laugh at the clowns and join in the seasonal play,
We'll shower our loved ones with overpriced gifts and heap overmuch food on their plate
And try to be nice to the people we meet and to neighbours and colleagues we hate.

So I'm Scrooge with a vengeance but it must be said that he was Dickensian too,
We still have the prisons' the workhouses gone' and still we are turning the screw,
The poor says the bible will always abide and money will not set them free,
And tinsel and baubles are not what they seem if they hang on a crude gallows tree.

I've scribbled and scribbled a whole year away and charted the hours and the days,
I've written of truth and I've perjured my soul in the lines of my ludicrous lays,
But something will stir me and tug at the veil like a wind that blows hard from the east,
And something of passion just cries for the page and batters my mind for release.

I wish you some pleasures, but most of all hope, and may you find peace in your days,
For all that I've said it's a wonderful world though we walk through a mystical maze,
Hold fast to your conscience, for all that you hear may well speak the needs of your heart.
And if you have charity bind it with love, and make each new-year a new start.

Dinosaurs

The dinosaur stood at the top of the hill,
Safe in the knowledge that all would be good,
There was plenty to look at and plenty to kill,
And the sun was still shining as always it should.

But out in the heavens a large piece of rock,
Was hurtling onward with increasing pace,
And our Tyrannosaurus was in for a shock,
When acres of mountain came crashing from space.

But tragedies happen and often as dire,
Though we look in amazement and can't comprehend,
When the leaders and prelates stand stoking the fire,
While the rest of us wonder just when will it end.

For now to the holylands fountain of peace,
The shame of the world carries armour and war,
The voice of the innocents scream for release,
As the flag of compassion is hurled to the floor.

My writ is not anger my wisdom not new,
I offer no answers to qualify pain,
I understand nothing of Arab or Jew,
But hatred is losing and loving is gain.

As I stand here a human and part of it all,
I will sigh for the beauty and hold back the tear,
For unlike the dinosaur I see the fall,
And all that is precious is grinding my fear.

When the mountain of Zion has crumbled to dust,
And the words of the prophet were ranted in-vain,
When the children of light find no reason to trust,
We will ask for princes of darkness to reign.

In Praise of Cynicism

Why don't we take in washing from the people down the road,
Share all we have with everyone and equalise the load,
Work only for a neighbour without want for pay or kind,
Hold all our land in commonwealth and equity of mind.

Provide a home and haven for the destitute and sick,
Cast down the towers and palaces save not a single brick,
Forswear the pride in magnitude let small have all the sway,
And as for all that money, why not give it all away.

The food in all the shops and stores, distribute far and wide,
With help from politicians who have never never lied,
Give dreams and hopes to children with no cause to shed a tear,
Knowing when the greed is gone there'll be no need for fear.

But I'm speaking like a communist a rebel and a red,
I'd best attempt just none of this and stay at home in bed,
I'll buy a bigger stereo and drown inside the noise,
And drink myself to happiness like all the other boys.

I'll start an e-mail company with CD ROM and disc,
And call it fleece-um-all dot com and never face a risk,
I'll lie and cheat and steal a bit to get straight to the top,
And till the taxman gets me I will never face the drop.

At last I'm feeling better I was nearly in a trance,
To think that there's a better way just wasn't worth a glance,
To all the good in having things I almost was quite blind,
But now I'm feeling quite myself, I'm back inside mankind.

Kind Hearts

If you live in the country by meadow and hill,
You watch how the animals rarely are still,
The hoofed and the horned things have quaint little ways,
To fill out the hours and pad out the days.

A cow is a creature with little to want,
No need for the college or baptismal font,
A stately progression from byre to the block,
McDonalds just waiting and watching the clock.

And when they are needy like girls on the pull,
They get the A.I. man and never the bull,
And though he smiles gently and has a nice name,
For the poor ruddy heifer it isn't the same.

The sheep by her own wants is top of the class,
She spends all her time eating serious grass,
One haircut a year and no work to be done,
The whole of her life is a bundle of fun.

But are they content I'm inclined to think not,
Yet they seem quite happy with what they have got,
With flystrike and scrapie to fill out the time,
The whole of existence is really sublime.

A Pony it seems is a burdensome thing,
He's rarely a Pegasus shorn of the wing,
There's hay in at one end and mulch at the tail,
And constant expense for the farriers nail.

With saddles and bridles and all sorts of tack,
Its down to the bank just to barrow it back,
And so you must spend like the prodigals curse,
Oh nil desperandum a racehorse is worse.

And so to the pigs that I frankly admire,
A coating of mud is a natty attire,
A fine flush of bristle not pompous or proud,
A generous being never gawky or loud.

I think to myself if the Buddhists are right,
To return and return when the old soul takes flight,
And though not the way of a prelate or prig,
For reincarnation please make me a pig.

I can see myself now as a pot bellied boar.
Just to wade in the wallow how could I want more,
With the old sow beside me two snouts in the bin,
A pot bellied popsey to succour my sin.

But fanciful notions are easy to write,
As I sit here content in the dark of the night,
While out in the moor there are lambs in the fold,
And the night duty shepherds stand stark in the cold.

I love my life here and would want for no change,
Where the kith and the kind are the safe and the strange,
The hoofed and the horned things are here but a while,
So learn as you watch them and watch as you smile.

Mendacity

St Fibbulus the Greater pours a blessing on the age,
The muse of politicians and of prelates and the stage,
He fills the lines of packaging each cranny every nook,
And every type of magazine each paper and each book.

St Fibbulus the Greater knows the child upon your knee,
He opens up the iron gate that sets the prisoner free,
The social science of tower blocks he laid most every brick,
And ponders with magicians as they form the newest trick.

St Fibbulus the Greater helps the salesman at your door,
He helps the erring doctor tell you just what lays in store,
The car mechanic knows him and he's in at the repair,
And thanks to him the caring trades are always always there.

St Fibbulus the Greater sees the start of every war,
He's first with the I love you and the profit of the whore,
He understands the need in man for anger and for pain,
And in the sweat of lovers' songs it's here he comes again.

St Fibbulus the Greater feels the start of each romance,
He holds you in his gentle grip the dancer and the dance,
The truest truth you ever know was written by his pen,
And he is sometime everything and all to all of men.

St Fibbulus the Greater carves his runes into the stone,
His essence creeps inside us into heart and blood and bone,
He is our inner covenant the secret parts within,
And who of all the sinners here would call his wisdom sin.

St Fibbulus the Greater is much needed by mankind,
To oil the wheels of industry to make the axe feel kind,
To tell a gentle story when the pain is far too real,
And to explain when reasons wit denies the way we feel.

St Fibbulus the Greater is a balm to rest the soul,
Where truth is pain this gentle saint can make the troubled whole,
Who cares what glories waited had we not endured the fall,
When great and good St Fibbulus makes fibbers of us all.

Oh B - - - - R

I bought a dog and called him Rover,
Rover bit me on the hand,
Told him he was very wicked
B - - - - r didn't understand.

Took him on a lead out shopping,
Rover bit me on the knee,
Thought I'd had enough of Rover,
Better set the B - - - - r free.

Drove him out onto the moorland,
Rover bit me causing pain,
In the car he snarled with anger,
Took the B - - - - r home again.

Took him to the Vet's for answers,
Rover bit me on the ear,
Vet amused at my reaction,
Said "never show the B - - - - r fear".

Walked the dog to passing circus,
Rover bit me on the thigh,
Felt at home for just a moment,
Cunning B - - - - r caught my eye.

Took him down to play with lions,
They bit Rover ' nothing left,
I went home with just a collar,
B - - - - rs gone I'm quite bereft.

Rover was a vicious B - - - - r,
Bit me nearly every day,
Still I'm sad and very lonely,
B o x e r dog has gone away.

Patrick And The Devil

He was drunk every morning as everyone knew,
He was drunk every evening as well,
And sure as tomorrow as everyone said,
Old Patrick was destined for hell.

The night before Christmas the wind it blew cold,
And Patrick sat home all alone,
When the devil came in through the living room wall,
Saying Patrick I've come for my own.

Said Pat to the devil I'm sure you're a man,
Who plays cards like a master no doubt,
So sit by the fire and drink for a while,
And lets play till the whisky runs out.

Said the devil to Patrick I'm sure you can see,
I have nothing on me but my skin,
And though you may wager with all that you own,
There is nothing from me you can win.

But there is now said Patrick you said when you came,
For you came to my house for your own,
If you win you take me with all that is here,
If I win you leave me alone.

Oh the devil the devil said whispering low,
This was never my usual way,
But bring out the glasses and rake up the fire,
And pour me a drink and I'll stay.

So Pat dealt the hand with the practice of years,
Three each for the devil and he,
Three kings shouts the devil its time we were off,
Three aces said Pat so I'm free.

Now Pat's full of virtue a model to men,
His temperament no longer dark,
Because every last sin has been blotted away,
And as every last card had a mark.

Progress

I stood on the fortification,
With the battle sound brave in my ear,
And my chieftain safe in the earthworks,
Sent me a flaming spear.

I threw the spear with a vengeance,
Not knowing where it would go,
And my liege lord safe in the castle keep,
Sent me an arrow and bow.

I fired the arrow skyward,
And looked to see what I'd done,
And my captain safe in the armoury,
Sent me the loaded gun.

I fired my gun from the trenches,
Wishing the day would pass,
And my general safe in a distant land,
Sent me the mustard gas.

I laid out the gas like a blanket,
Over Passchendaele Ypres and the Somme,
And my scientist safe in his ivory tower,
Sent me the nuclear bomb.

I dropped my bomb on the city,
And mankind felt the searing pain,
Then no-one was safe in the whole wide world,
And never will be again.

Road Kill. or 'A Lapin Lament'

I was driving down the highway and with nothing on my mind,
The traffic moving slowly and with quite a queue behind,
When a rabbit with a death wish or a suicidal bent,
Came rushing from the hedgerow and beneath my wheels it went.

The bump it raised the front wheel and then the rear one too,
And stopping rather quickly I first wondered what to do,
Concluding that I must at least make sure that it was dead,
I wandered down the tarmac to the growing stain of red.

The suicidal rabbit had succeeded in its aim,
The wheels I checked were quite intact, the bodywork the same,
And then I noticed curiously that littered here and there,
Were the fur and feathered bodies of the common and the rare.

In one place was a badger with his teeth bared in a smile,
A weasel lay in cold repose and he'd been there a while,
A brace of pheasants, 'separate' had played their little game,
And here a sort of something that I simply couldn't name.

I pondered that were things so bad that fauna from the field,
Were coming to the highway for their little lives to yield,
Were they waiting up the banking behind each bush and stump,
The manic hare the half crazed fox just waiting there to jump.

I walked back to my vehicle the thought still in my head,
I drove to work down country lanes and counted up the dead,
A hedgehog here a tomcat there a pigeon rook and crow,
It seems these rural suicides are everywhere I go.

A call to the Samaritans, perhaps the N.F.U.,
E-Mail the R.S.P.C.A and find out what to do,
This carnage cannot go unchecked, cry scandal to the air,
Am I the only motorist with mind enough to care.

For soon it will be sheep and cows all getting in the act,
The horses and the threatened breeds will form a solemn pact,
Then deer and pigs will all unite and leap from walls and trees,
The traffic of society brought swiftly to its knees.

But then I'm playing mind games and these dead are best forgot,
They just clutter up the highway and they lay there till they rot,
So I squashed another rabbit just a lapin fading star,
And I'm glad it wasn't anything that wrecked the bloody car.

Suffrage

He rapped on the door in a purposeful way,
Then the letterbox rattled as well,
And I watched as he shuffled from garden to step,
While he jabbed and he pushed at the bell.

I answered; he stood there, both fixed eye to eye,
For a notch on his clipboard to claim,
And while under my breath I regretted the move,
He addressed me by number and name.

He said Mr Grant, which I knew wasn't right,
His salute made with culture and care,
As you see I'm the candidate here for your vote,
If you just have a moment to spare.

The smile was as bright as the gleaming rosette,
Well formed for the Westminster way,
And he knew that I'd listen or thought that I should,
So he started the act of his play.

I'll labour for you in conservative ways,
With a bright green aside to my trying,
A democrat born formed of liberal clay,
While all of the others are lying.

I can promise you all that you ever might need,
Be it pensions, the law or your health,
For remember the other lot don't care a fig,
And will drastically damage your wealth.

I looked at him, captured him, cast him aside,
At least with my mind and my reason,
And as hot air floats upward he drifted away,
Like a dandelion seed in the season.

For the cynic inside me was struck by the joke,
And my laughter cut through his oration,
A clown in his colours with little to say,
Who someday will govern our nation.

The Seven Deadliest And All That

And do you have that dreadful place,
Where comforts care can find no trace,
When dreamless nights are nightmare cold,
And runes are cast where tales are told.

The cloven feet that trot behind,
And beat their pace into your mind,
Where stygian demons laud your fame,
And heap their praise upon your name.

The sin of pride may damn your soul,
And paint your heart as black as coal,
The lies we tell both black and white,
Will send us to eternal night.

Can gluttony the final feast,
Still tie us firmly to the beast,
While avarice that timely friend,
Will surely get us in the end.

And venting anger must be great
For sealing firmly hope and fate,
A lapse to lust may set you free,
But does it make a better me.

If greed is bad tell me I'm wrong,
For I'm the singer of the song,
The advertisers write the words,
To pacify the envious herds.

But sloth has got me in its grip,
The steersman of my little ship,
A laurel bed my resting place,
A mendicant of pure disgrace.

I've counted seven maybe eight,
To each and all I can relate,
I don't dispute I've seen the fall,
But tend to just enjoy them all.

But there's the rub or so it seems,
They still come back to haunt my dreams
And somewhere in my dreadful place,
The smile is slipping from my face.

The trotting hooves are close behind,
And beat their rhythm in my mind,
The thing that follows counts each pace
And sets the mood for time and space.

If god there is, if god there be,
Forgive the sins of little me,
Thus be it said that I have tried,
And loved and lusted lied and died.

Trolling

Darwin said all things evolve,
And this I hold as true,
And people who deny this fact,
Just haven't got a clue.

And what is fact in birds and bees,
Is fact in fabled things,
Of goblins, gremlins, elves and such,
Of fays and fairy rings.

For in this technological age,
When all is new and brash,
The little folk have too evolved,
To rob us of our cash.

What other reason could derive,
The faults in man made things,
In motors, mixers, microwaves,
In sofas, shoes and springs.

It cannot be we get it wrong,
No fault in mans great wit,
A sprite to wreck the dishwasher,
Or make the part not fit.

The gremlin in the desktop,
Has caused my rhymes to fail,
It couldn't be the way I type,
That wrecks my little tale.

And what about the car I drive,
The elves they know each part,
That's why on winter mornings,
The ruddy thing won't start.

They're in most all the merchandise,
Technologists provide,
It's that or all the warranties,
And guarantees have lied.

They're why our flights are oft delayed,
They're why the trains are late,
They're why at times the phones won't work,
We're in a sorry state.

Perhaps we have invited them,
By saying they're not there,
To bring confusion to a world,
And raise us to despair.

So please beware the little folk,
They lurk in each device,
As cunning as the scientist,
As secretive as mice.

Be certain they are everywhere,
In kettle car and cot,
And better we remember those,
Our reasoned world forgot.

Twelfth Night.

Its almost twelfth night and I'm feeling quite sad,
Said the fairy on top of the tree,
When your way past fifty it quite gets you mad,
When you see what they're doing to me.
Hauled out every Christmas and tied to a twig,
It's hardly a yearly surprise,
And I'm not even dusted, they don't care a fig,
So what would a poor girl surmise?

Though festooned with glitter, I'll not be profane,
I will stick to the seasonal cheer,
For once every twelve month I'm stuck here again,
From December right through to New Year.
The tatty old robin is fading with age,
His feathers a lustreless brown,
And he never says nothing, a real empty page,
Still I smile, though I'd much rather frown.

The lights start to flicker, another blown fuse,
The holly wreath dries on the door,
The left over turkey makes seven-day stews,
And the pine needles heap on the floor,
And I think of the past years when first I was made,
When my wings were as bright as the moon,
Of days full of laughter not like this charade,
The days that have faded too soon.

But I have seen love in the mind of a man,
And the joy of a woman who cares,
For she knows that in all he does all that he can,
And thus will do all that he dares,
So as I'm put back in the box once again,
With the trinkets and baubles so bright,
There's a thought that goes with me a year to sustain,
And to warm in the darkest of night.

We all have our treasure though be it so small,
And we all have a soul and a heart,
When we love one another we answer a call,
And no anger can force us apart,
If we hold to each other we grow day by day,
While we sail on an uncharted sea,
Horizons are only an embrace away,
And I know they are even for me.

Vote Vote Vote

Is this then the year of political sense,
As parties presume we are dullards and dense,
They cavort and confuse us in infinite measure,
And prattle and pose for electoral pleasure.

For we as receivers must stand in the herd,
And listen intent to each mendacious word,
The lies and the libels each slander and curse,
A vote for confusion or something much worse.

I'd be much forgiven should I now assert,
That limited truth is not able to hurt,
That bold innuendo is only a ploy,
And democracy reigns as the top tyrants toy.

To me they're the same with a differing flag,
They each think the populace safe in the bag,
They all play with race and they argue on tax,
And never allow we poor sods to relax.

I'm sick to the back teeth of all that I'm told.
The bright and the earnest the fools and the bold,
They vie for my vote and they play on my greed,
And don't give a fig for the people in need.

For in the analysis what can be said,
If its all death and taxes then better be dead,
This whole life's a gamble of aces and jacks,
And the railway of life has just bounced off the tracks.

Oh joy for the ballot box, joy for the vote,
For let me not sound a dissentient note,
We get what we ask for and what we deserve,
We vote in the servant and then we all serve.

An absolute monarch, a god given king,
It has an attraction and positive ring,
A Cromwell or Warwick to give us the lead,
With the barons to please and the peasants to bleed.

But I see no difference dictators will rise,
Its just we elect to the ultimate prize,
We call him prime minister, what's in a name,
He's just a slick spiv who's ahead of the game.

But then that's democracy tooth fang and claw,
We get what we shout for and nothing much more,
But I am content with the certain and true,
That I can blame all of this damned mess on you.

Wizardry

The wizard of wizards stands high on the hill,
In the chill and the still of the air,
And he casts for a spell that could shatter the stars,
And would set the whole world in his snare.

The wizard of wizards is gnarled as an oak,
Though his skin is the colour of milk,
And he's dressed for the wind as it blows from the west,
In the mantle of raven wing silk.

But out in the badlands the spirits of sand,
Are as wise as the wizard is strong,
For the fey of the desert are old as the moon,
Weaving mists with their dew scented song.

The wizard of wizards has raised his great staff,
As the thunderclouds gather apace,
And he laughs as the desert folk shelter below,
And the wild lightening pictures his face.

For the eagle at war is a terrible thing,
When the wizard of wizards has sway,
When the lion is following clutching the sword,
What more might the poor do but pray.

A voice for the children, a cry for the damned,
To the wizard with hands on his ears,
The gathering anger that's rounding the world,
And the blood that cries soft bitter tears.

I was born as the bombs fell and though not to blame,
My silence will not give me peace,
For if I say nothing I fire the gun,
And where may I go for release.

They may have the truth of it, I do not know,
But peace is as precious as light,
And there still may be magic in staying the hand,
Where our hope is as cunning as might.

Printed in the United Kingdom
by Lightning Source UK Ltd.
132451UK00001B/352-378/P